DREAMIN' ALONG WITH THE BAY CITIES

Most folk've got a favourite dream they conjure up when they're feeling a bit down . . . and the Bay City Rollers are no exception! So we thought we'd get in on their secret dreams . . .

WOODY's a dreamer all right. At school, he was always being told off for day-dreaming. Now, when he's relaxin', he often drifts off somewhere . . . like sunny Jamaica! And we wouldn't mind goin' with him, that's for sure. ALAN's a bit of a wild dreamer, too. When he was younger he always dreamed of being . . . a star musician! Now he dreams of being a farmer . . . we'll see!

continued on next page

To Helen from Mum & Dad. XMAS 1975

3

£1.15

BAY CITIES

ERIC dreams about travellin'.
He's always on the move,
and never wants to stop. The
sky's the limit!
LES dreams of bein' a wild
adventurer, and gettin' up to
all sorts of wild stunts.
The others always have to
step in 'n' control him. And
his pet dream? Riding off
into the sunset in a blue
Mustang.
DEREK's dreams are just
the sort of everyday, normal
fantasies you'd expect! He
just wants to be rich and
happy with the most beautiful
girl he can find — and
thousands of adoring fans,
too — of course!

HOW STRONG WILLED ARE YOU?

Can you resist temptation ? Are you good at keeping your word ? Do you break promises ? Are *you* a strong willed person ? That's what we're gonna find out ! Nearly everyone decides to do something good at sometime or other, or to change their ways. But many of us are too weak-willed to carry them out to the full. Are you really like that, or are you a strong willed person who can adjust to changes when you want to ? Let's see . . .

1 *Along comes January the first. Time to make a New Year Resolution. We all make them. Do we keep them ? Your resolution is that you will study hard, every night, even weekends. WOW! How long could you keep it up for ?*

- a. A day ?
- b. A week ?
- c. A month ?
- d. A year ?

2 *Mum's been complaining a lot lately about the untidy state of your room. How you never tidy it up, always leaving it to her, and she is busy enough, etc., etc. So you decide to help her in the home. How often will you help ?*

- a. When you think of it ?
- b. Once a month ?
- c. Once a week ?
- d. Daily ?

3 *You are out with your friends and you over-hear one say to another, "She's getting a bit plump lately." They are referring to YOU! The horrible fact is, that they are right. You have been over eating, and are a bit plump. Dieting is the only answer. How long can you keep it up ?:*

- a. Until you reach your target ?
- b. A whole month ?
- c. A whole week ?
- d. A whole day ?

4 There is a fab dress in the boutique near your home — you fall in love with it as soon as you set eyes on it. But, wow, what a price! No forthcoming birthday, or Christmas. You will just have to earn the money for the dress. Next door, they are advertising for a paper girl. Hello, paper girl — but for how long ?:

a. Until you have enough money to buy the dress ?
b. A week ?
c. A morning ?
d. Change your mind ?

5 You have found your Christmas present hidden. There it is wrapped in Christmas paper with a label on it. It is weeks before Christmas day. It is a big, exciting parcel. You have no idea what is in it. It doesn't rattle. How long can you wait before you open it ?

a. Until Christmas ?
b. Keep popping back to look at it ?
c. Wait a week then take a peek ?
d. Peek at it straight away ?

6 You are playing in a hockey match. At least three times in the first half, while you are in possession of the ball, your opposite number on the other side, hooks your feet from under you with her hockey stick. Soon you get the chance to do that same thing to her. How long can you resist the temptation ?:

a. Resist it completely ?
b. Wait until next time ?
c. Trip her up ?
d. Do it again ?

HOW TO SCORE:

a = 20 points. b = 15 points. c = 10 points. d = 5 points.

So how did you do?

105 to 120:
If you got the highest score then you aren't as strong willed as you thought you were. No one is that perfect. Not even you! It could be you set too many high standards — and can't live up to them.

70-100:
Well done! You are the most strong willed of us all. You have the strength of will to assess your character and be honest when doing a quiz like this. Good for you! But can you keep it up ? Let's hope so ! Good luck.

35-65:
That's more like it. No one is perfect as we've already said. We all have weaknesses. You seem to know yours. How about trying to do something about them? Try willing yourself to be a stronger person. Go on, try HARD!

under 30:
Oh dear! You really think the worst of yourself. Are you really that weak willed ? Can't be bothered, eh ? See if you can try and make some positive decisions occasionally. There is room for improvement, isn't there ?

Patty's World

10

Like a pop star on holiday in Spain, perhaps . . .

WOW, THIS REQUEST FROM A LONELY LITTLE DOLLY SURE INSPIRES ME . . .

So first an L.P. all about me . . .

FUNNY LITTLE FRECKLE FACE . . . FED UP WITH THE HUMAN RACE . . . THAT'S PATTY

Then . . .

BECAUSE OF YOU, BABY, I'M NUMBER ONE! READY FOR OUR DATE?

BEEN READY FOR YEARS! ' HEY, MUM, WHO SAID EXCITEMENT WOULDN'T COME KNOCKING AT MY DOOR?

But the trouble with him being top of the pops would be . . .

Like . . . .

GRAB THAT MESSAGE IN THE BOTTLE, BOY, WHILE I KEEP THE CROCS AT BAY!

. . . ALL HIS OTHER FANS! I'D GET SHOVED IN THE BACKGROUND AGAIN IN NO TIME! SO I'D RATHER MY BOTTLE FLOATED TO WHERE THERE WEREN'T LOADS OF OTHER GIRLS . . .

WELL, SHE WOULDN'T BE BORED WITH THIS SCENE, EH, FELLAS?
And, maybe, one night in the Wimpy . . .
OOOH!
YOU PUT MY FRIEND DOWN, YOU BIG APE!
I wouldn't be all that keen to be treated like hunted prey, either . . .
DON'T YOU KNOW THERE'S A LAW AGAINST KIDNAPPING?
YOURS TRULY OBEYS ONLY THE LAW OF THE JUNGLE, SWEETHEART!
GREAT THAT YOU'RE A GIRL WITH SPIRIT THOUGH! TAMING YOU WILL BE A PLEASURE, PATTY!
YOU GO AN' JUMP IN THE SWAMP! I'M GETTING THE NEXT CANOE OUT OF HERE, TARZAN!
SO, ON SECOND THOUGHTS, PLEASE, BOTTLE, DON'T DRIFT OFF TO DARKEST AFRICA!
It didn't either, 'cos suddenly . . .
OH! THAT FISHERMAN HAS COLLARED IT!

13

BE A KNOW

We're always gettin' sack loads of letters from you lot wanting to know all kinds of things 'bout your heart throbs — so we thought it was about time we put some of your questions to the lads themselves. So grab yer note book and a pen and take full advantage of our question time . . . !

Q You always look so happy, Donny — but surely you get those days when things seem to hit rock bottom and all the sunshine in your life turns to clouds?

Liz — 14

A *You're right, Liz — of course I get those days. I wouldn't be human if I didn't, would I? But it's times like these when having good mates and a loving happy family steps right in 'n' helps you out! You know, I could'nt possibly stay glum for long with Jimmy clownin' around and Marie pulling my leg!*

Q I know jealousy is a horrible emotion, but do you ever feel jealous about things or people?

Mary — 15

A *'Course I do Mary. I'm only human aren't I? But I do try and control it. I'm not naturally a jealous kinda person, which makes things easier, but whenever I do feel the twinges I start telling myself how stupid I'm being and more than often it goes away! I always think that, like fear, once something like that gets a hold of you, it starts eating away at you. Bit of mind over matter works wonders y'know when you try hard!*

Q I know this is a bit of a cheeky question Woody, but what was your first date like. Were you nervous 'n' shy at all?

Sue — 14

A *I remember my first date vividly, Sue. It was disastrous! For starters I was so scared of Sally that I could hardly pluck up the courage to talk to her properly, let alone hold her hand and whisper sweet nothings. Then when we got in the cinema I took the plunge and put my arm round her, jogging her ice-cream all over her blouse. I nearly died!*

ALL!

Q When did you first become interested in drumming and the music business in general?

Janet — 12

A *Way back as far as I can remember I was fascinated by music and the things that surrounded it.*

Luckily I wasn't the only one in my family who caught the bug 'cos Alan was as crazy as me.

We got our first band together when we were at school — and we've never looked back!

Q When you're feelin' tensed up and tired after a hectic BCR tour what do you do to relax?

Lyn — 14

A *Well Lyn, you're right, I do get a bit over-tired sometimes and feel the need to get away. Not that I don't get on with the rest of the lads, of course! But even the best of friends need a rest from each other — so when I feel like that I pack up me camping gear, go and find a beautiful country spot and pitch a tent! I'm soon as good as new!*

Q When you were hard up and out of work in the East End of London did you ever feel like giving up your dreams of becoming a singer and actor?

Paula — 15

A *I must admit, Paula, I used to get pretty low sometimes — but never low enough to give up. Things have a funny way of turning up and changing your whole life when everything is bad, and that's what used to happen to me. I always knew that you need stickability in this business and I could never imagine me doing anything but what I'm doing now, so I had plenty of reserves in determination!*

Q. I know you lot are a right load of jokers and crazy things must happen to you all the time, but can you remember the most awkward 'n' embarrassing thing?

Jackie — 12

A. *Cor! The time I wore these extra tight trousers I had 'specially made was pretty bad. I'd just gone into a restaurant with the rest of the lads and was about to sit down when there was a horrible r-r-ripping noise.*

You've guessed! There was an enormous hole in 'em.?I don't think anybody else in the restaurant would have noticed, but the rest of the lads soon let 'em know with their roars of laughter!

Q I think you look great in your glitter gear Gary, honest, but my mum reckons you look a bit daft. Don't you ever feel stupid about going round in the kinda clothes you do?

Jenny — 13

A *The answer is definitely no — I never feel silly in my outfits, but your mum has got a point. I mean, she's as entitled to have views and tastes in clothes the same as I am. Our tastes are just completely different, that's all. I've always enjoyed dressin' up and lookin' unusual. Goin' shopping for clothes is one of my favourite pastimes and I always keep my eyes open for way-out gear.*

Anyway, I'm glad you like the things I wear!

HAVE YOU GOT YOUR LIFE ON A STRING..?

Are you the kinda girl who seems to make everything work out just the way you want, or does everything you tackle go wrong? In case you don't know already, have a bash at our quiz 'n' find out ..!

1. You're at a party when you spot a fella on the other side of the room that you've been swooning over for the past year! Now's your chance to pounce . . , Do you:
a. Slip upstairs and have a fit of nerves trying to pluck up courage to go and talk to him.
b. Put on your best sleezy walk and slink over towards him, dropping your hanky as you go.
c. Send your mate over to do the ground work, risking the fact that she might take a fancy to him in the process?
2. You've had a really hectic week and have planned an early night, but your Aunty rings up and asks if you'll baby-sit for her. Do you:
a. Tell her straight away that you're so tired you must go to bed early.
b. Get your nighty and toothbrush together and tell her you'll be round as long as you can stay the night.
c. Try and persuade your sister/brother/Mum to do it?
3. As usual you're in a frantic rush because you're late for a date, and in your haste you flick mascara all over your blouse. Do you:
a. Spend hours trying to rub it off with soapy water, making it worse.
b. Calmly get another top out of your cupboard that goes with the outfit, that you've been keepin' clean 'n' pressed in case of emergencies.
c. Stand your fella up 'cos you haven't got anything to wear?
4. You've seen a gorgeous dress in your local boutique that you really want. Trouble is your mate wants it too! Do you:
a. Nip down and see the assistant and ask her to put it by for you while you borrow some money.
b. Let your mate get it.
c. Spend hours trying to persuade her that it doesn't suit her?

5. You're merrily waltzing down the street when Paul from next door (who looks like David Essex) bumps into you. His greeting words are: "What on earth have you done to your face?" Putting your finger on your cheek you discover a false eye lash!
Do you:
a. Quickly say, "Furry cheeks are all the rage now, Paul . . . !"
b. Go bright red and quickly pull it off.
c. Start giggling!
6. Your favourite group comes to your town to do a concert, and the queue for tickets is miles long. Do you:
a. Give up straight away and tell yourself that you can go next time they come round.
b. Pay little brother 10p to go and queue for a ticket for you.
c. Go and queue yourself!
7. You've planned a special trip with a mate one Saturday, but right at the last minute she rings up to tell you that she's laid up in bed with a bout of flu. Do you:
a. Decide to eat your packed lunch at home and skulk around all day 'cos you haven't got anything to do.
b. Nip round and see your mate at the risk of catchin' it yourself.
c. Ring up another mate and see if she can make it instead.

SCORE
1. a0, b10, c5.
2. a0, b10, c5.
3. a5, b10, c0.
4. a10, b0, c5.
5. a10, b0, c5.
6. a0, b10, c5.
7. a0, b5, c10.

HOW DID YOU DO?

0-25

Oh, c'mon . . . things don't seem to work out very well for you, that's true, but you don't make much of an effort to get things running smoothly . . . and in your direction! You always seem to take things on the chin when a problem comes your way or you're forced to make a decision.

A lot of your trouble could be put to your lackin' confidence . . . so c'mon — try and forget what other folk think about you! Life doesn't just run itself, y'know — you have to make it work out the way you want it, so try going into things with a more optimistic, vigorous attitude and you'll be surprised what comes your way!

30-50

You've those strings in your hands most of the time, haven't you?, but the trouble is they tend to get a bit tangled at the very worse times! Then you wonder why you feel so cheesed off! You just have

to make your mind up more positively 'bout just what you do want, don't you?

You tend to get half-way into makin' things work out your way, and then back out at the last minute just as you're winning! Don't be afraid to go full out for what you want . . . as long as you're not hurting or shoving anybody else out in in the meantime!

55-70

Congratulations . . . you really have got your life on a string, and it makes things much more fun doesn't it. Bein' able to make things work out so you usually get the best end of the deal can also be an advantage in lotsa other ways too . . . savin' energy 'n' time f'rinstance! One warning tho' — you tend to be a bit pushy when it comes to getting your own way sometimes, and you sacrifice other folk's feelings so a situation will turn out to your advantage!

WELL SEASONED'

Follow our tips for your wardrobe right through the year. Just start with the basics and gradually add the extras. After all wardrobe planning is what fashion's all about!

WINTER

A warm winter coat is an essential during the cold months, so make sure you pick one that will go with the rest of your wardrobe — and especially with your accessories. Choose a classic shape for a coat that will last and last.

There's plenty of rain about all during the year but especially in the winter so something to keep it out wouldn't be a bad idea. Whatever type of mac you choose make sure it's waterproof — oh, and don't forget that warm woolly hat, cosy mitts and a brolly!

Finally who could go through the winter without a fur? The fakes are just as good as the real thing and a lot cheaper too! And nothing could be more cuddlier and cosy to keep those cold winds at bay. So make sure you find your fur and stick to it — you just couldn't do better!

SPRING

WELL SEASONED'

When spring comes along, out come all the flowers and out come all those light, bright sunny clothes again.

SPRING

When Spring comes along it's time to start thinking about all those lovely T-shirts again — great!

And dresses too — you know, those pretty knee-length ones that you can wear anywhere, and still look good when you pop a cardi over the top.

That fashionable two-piece is also perfect for your Spring wardrobe, 'cos when the sun's shining you can wear it on its own, but when it gets a bit nippy you can pop a woolly underneath and still come up smilin'!

SUMMER

Summer is the most feminine time of the year — so pull out those long, long skirts and sunny tops!

Pick a pretty back baring top and a long long skirt for the start of your summer wardrobe and really feel like a girl for a change!

Frilled layers are also something that couldn't be prettier and don't forget a sunny little hat too, it just adds that extra bit of summer!

A pair of fresh white trousers are a must for your summer wardrobe — nothing looks so cool on those sun-baked days. A cotton blouse always looks good too, and you can wear that with trousers or skirts!

AUTUMN

'WELL SEASONED'
AUTUMN

After the heat of summer it's nice to get back to cosy colours and clothes again so make the most of 'em autumn days!

Cardi's are an autumn must whether you wear 'em over trousers or a neat skirt. Who'd be without one?

FASHION FORECAST '76

Autumn dresses are great for a date or for granny so be sure of yours for those "I don't know what to wear" days!

Finally — jeans. We wear 'em all year round — and we bet you do too!

END OF SEASON

DAVID
ESSEX

23

HOME SWEET

You don't need to spend a fortune to make your room homely . . . . and pretty! Here are a few simple ideas for you to make. You can vary them

SUPER SCRAPS !

Patchwork is a great idea, 'cos it uses up all your old scraps of materials. You can start off with a sewing bag or cushion to experiment, and build up to a bedspread! First of all, decide on a basic shape. Squares,

diamonds or hexagons are the best. Then cut yourself a basic pattern in stiff cardboard — or, if you're taking it up seriously, you can buy plastic patterns ('templates') at lots of sewing shops. Now cut out all your little patches — allowing $\frac{1}{4}$" all round for turnings. For a cushion we suggest 2" squares . . . that should be simple enough to start you off.

SCENTED SACHETS

. . . What could be nicer to hang in your bedroom or wardrobe to brighten things up and make the air smell lovely 'n' fresh. Especially if you made 'em yourself!

If you're lucky enough to have some lavender bushes in your

garden — or rosemary — you've got it made! If not, you can get dried lavender from chemists. Not only do lavender bags make your clothes smell good — but they can look gorgeous too.

The basic idea is very simple. You just need small scraps of pretty material. We used bright felt (you can buy small squares of it very cheaply) and scraps of floral prints. Stock up with some lace and ribbon to trim them . . . and off you go! 'Pink'(!) the edges of the felt, for a pretty effect, with pinking shears. Once you've made the bag, just turn it the right way out, fill it with lavender (or rosemary), and tie it up with ribbon. The smell lasts for years, and makes your clothes smell great!

HOME

to suit yourself—and add your own individual touch!

Now just start stitching them together! (Remembering to alternate your colours and patterns of material for variety.) It's easier if you first gather the material along the edges, and pull it in around the cardboard pattern. This keeps the edges straight while you're joining them together!

As an extra detail, you can embroider along some of the seams on the plain squares. You could make a life work of it, and end up with a patchwork quilt!

STRIKE A LIGHT !

Like our lovely lampshade? You'll feel very proud of having made it yourself! You'll need $\frac{1}{2}$ yd. 36 in. wide material (we chose cotton gingham).

You'll also want $\frac{1}{2}$ yd. of lace or patterned braiding — and a round lampshade frame from Woolworth's or use an old one of Mum's.)

For this, you fold the material in half and stitch the raw edges together, making it into a tube. Then turn it the right way out. Turn the top edge in over the frame, and stitch it in place with a $\frac{1}{2}$ in. turning.

Now attach the lace to the bottom edge—turning the raw edge under as you do it (the fabric should be hanging about 2 in. below the bottom of the frame.) Now just sew a running stitch around the shade, where it touches the bottom of the frame. Pull it in — and to finish, tie some ribbon round it!

FREE SAMPLE !

The Victorian revival's really spreading now. Here in the Pink office we've all been busy with our embroidery samplers, boasting 'HOME SWEET HOME', 'PATIENCE IS A VIRTUE' and other words of wisdom. They're really fun to do once you get started, so why not have a try? Choose lots of pretty colours to work with — do borders of flowers around them as well if you're 'into' embroidery: a chance to really show your skill!

They look really flash framed and hanging on the wall. Get yourself some fairly basic material — linen, or an open-weave fabric for cross-stitch. Work out — on paper first! — your design, then lightly copy it on to the material in pencil.

You can always try to develop it as you go along, but it's best to start off with a basic plan. Have a look at ours to get some ideas — then let your imagination run wild!

Carla, Don't Cry!

Carla wasn't with the East Brothers' West African tour just because she worked for a music magazine — for a long time now, she'd been Don East's best girlfriend. But, in Ghana's capital, Accra . . .

SWEET MUSIC, HUH?

EVERYTHING'S SWEET HERE — EVEN THE DISTANT SURF'S BOOMING AWAY AS GOOD AS A PERCUSSION GROUP! STILL, WORK CALLS — TIME I TOOK SOME PICS!

DARN THAT MAN, HE'S WALKED RIGHT INTO MY SHOT OF DON AND HAL — WELL, IT WON'T BE A PICTURE OF A HAPPY FACE, ANYWAY!

27

28

.30

HOME LOVIN'

THERE'S never any family friction between the younger generation and Ma and Pa Osmond. If there's any disagreement then the whole family sit down and talk it out sensibly !

Although Donny loves globe-trottin' and visiting new countries he loves to get home . . . home to see his mates and to get stuck in to some of his hobbies again. After all, you can hardly cart a room full of electrical gear half-way round the world!
Even though some of the Osmonds are married and living away from home (Alan, Wayne and Merrill all live next to each other in identical houses !) the family still meet up for a full-sized "family meal" very frequently !

(*Please turn to page* 34.)

BOYS

The Osmonds love touring and meeting their fans...but they also like it when they can just relax on their ranch in Utah as one big happy family. After all, there's no place like home, is there . . . ?

HOME LOVIN' BOYS

When the family have finished their mammoth meal they don't just go and watch the T.V.! — Oh no, they play fun games like charades or have a little sing-song! Y'see Ma and Pa Osmond believe in the old fashioned family ways when folk used to amuse themselves. Not that the lads or Marie object . . . they reckon they get far more laughs from playin' daft games and relating funny stories than sittin' glued to the telly!

ROLL ON!

Being a Bay City Roller is a pretty time-consuming job but every now and again the lads get a spare couple of days to do exactly what they want..!

ERIC *likes to keep himself fit with a quick game of football.* Woody *is a watery kinda fella tho' — there's nothing he loves better than to go swimming!* Derek *enjoys a good gallop on a trusty steed, while* Lesley *loves to fiddle around with electronics when he's got some spare time and* Alan's *a bit of an artist! Give him a paintbrush and canvas and he's well away!*

The Good fairy

CHRISTMAS Eve is just about the nicest day of the year for fairies.

All the rest of the year they're running about replacing teeth with sixpences (or is it 10p now?), making people feel happy, sad, or even bad-tempered and doing fairy-type things like that. Yeah, they have a pretty busy time, fairies . . .

But the day before Christmas is different. Christmas Day they have to work over-time, y'see, so Christmas Eve is their day off—and they deserve it.

After all, they're only little folk, y'know. You and me, we have at least three or four weeks off a year, but them, they only get the one day, so they make the most of it.

They look forward to putting on their best gear — gossamer wings and the like — forget all about the good, and naughty, deeds they usually have to do, and off they flit, dropping in on old friends, hob-nobbing in the fairy glens and supping the old thistle-down wine. Fairies really know how to enjoy themselves when they get the chance.

What's that I hear you say? You don't, believe in fairies? Well, a lot of people don't y'know. It's kind of gone out of fashion, which is a pity really.

Karen didn't believe in fairies either. In fact, she never even thought about them much. Right now she was more concerned with Steve, her boyfriend, or, rather, her ex-boyfriend. She was having problems, see.

Everything had been all right up until a few days ago and then they'd gone to that party. She hadn't wanted to go because somehow she'd had a feeling that something was going to go wrong. And it did. To start with they had a bit of a tiff:

"What's wrong with you," Steve said, "you've been down in the dumps ever since we got here. If you didn't fancy it you shouldn't have come . . ."

"What? And leave you to go out by yourself? No fear . . ."

"Oh, Karen, don't you trust me even a little bit? I'm not going to rush off with somebody else just because you're not here, give me a bit more credit." And Steve had taken her by the shoulders and looked into her eyes.

That was when the girl walked in. Karen had never seen her before—she would have remembered if she had because she was the kind of girl you couldn't forget. She had a mass of long silky blond hair, enormous green eyes and the kind of figure that you usually see modelling clothes in a magazine. She was very beautiful. Steve had noticed her too. And Karen noticed him noticing . . .

CONTINUED ON PAGE 38

She felt herself go all cold inside and she stiffened, turning away so that she didn't have to look at Steve's face.

"Come on, let's dance," he said and she knew he was just trying to edge nearer to that girl. The girl knew too and she was smiling, confident and cool.

Karen had already made up her mind what she was going to do and that's why she suddenly turned and ran. Running away from that room, from the girl—and from Steve. Running away because she suddenly felt unsure, insecure and, most of all, jealous.

All that was a week ago now but Karen still remembered it vividly. She hadn't seen Steve since and when he rang, which he often did, her pride wouldn't allow her to talk to him. How could he, how could he do that—to her?

And now it was Christmas Eve. She'd always been excited about Christmas before but, this year, it didn't seem as if she was going to enjoy it at all.

It wasn't the same if you didn't have someone you loved to share it with. Oh, there was Mum and Dad and the family, but . . .

Outside it was cold but as Karen stepped out on to the frost-hard pavement she didn't notice the icy wind and the yellow-grey sky threatening snow. Hands deep in her pockets she walked fast, looking ahead but not really seeing. She must have walked miles because the next thing she knew she was out of the town and in the middle of a wood, kicking up the brown leaves and looking for somewhere to sit down. She found a log and plonked down, head in hands.

"Looks like it's going to snow."

Karen looked round. Perched on the other end of the log was a child, so small that its feet feet swung several inches off the ground. A girl or a boy, it was difficult to tell. The angelic face was surrounded by a halo of golden hair on top of which rested a circle of woodland leaves and flowers, slightly askew and now being pushed roughly back into place by a plump hand. The child wore only a thin dress which seemed to be— but it was impossible—spun round the chubby figure.

Karen shivered, feeling cold just looking at the bare hands and feet. What on earth was a young child doing out here dressed like that? Never mind, it was none of her business. Right now she didn't care that much about anybody but herself.

"I'm sorry," she started, "I didn't see you there. Don't worry, I'll go away if you'd rather . . ."

"Oh no, don't worry about me," the voice was surprisingly mature, "I could do with some company, nobody seems to want me around nowadays."

"Going to a fancy dress?" Karen asked brightly, it seemed the only logical conclusion.

"Nope," the child edged nearer along the log and Karen decided that the face was definitely female, it was so pretty.

"Aren't you rather cold," Karen offered her scarf.

The child pushed it away scornfully. "Fairies don't get cold."

Karen smiled. "Maybe not, but sometimes we humans do, here . . ."

"I'm not human!" The little girl looked

positively outraged. "I'm a fairy. I'll show you my wings if you like."

Karen suppressed a giggle.

"Actually, it's my wings that give me most trouble," the little girl continued seriously. "They're so beautiful you see, that all the others get jealous.

Can I help it if I've got beautiful wings? I didn't ask for them, they just grew like that. But the others don't see it like that, they just get jealous—won't even let me go and see them in case I show them up. So I'm stuck here on Chrsitmas Eve with no-one to go and see . . . and on Christmas Eve of all days . . ."

"Well we all get jealous sometimes," Karen sighed, "it's so stupid but you can't help it, it just happens. And it makes you do the silliest things as well. I suppose we just don't like to think that we're not the prettiest, most intelligent person there is . . ."

★   ★   ★

"You know, of course, that it's all the bad fairies' fault," the child leant forward confidentially, "they're the ones who get humans into trouble. They just love upsetting them.

"You see, sometimes fairies are good and sometimes they're bad. I don't know why, we're just made like that. My friend Oriel's really terrible.

"Do you know, the other day she got inside this girl at a party—we fairies do that, you see, get inside people and tell them to do nice or horrible things—anyway, Oriel got inside this girl and told her to be jealous, she even made her walk out on her boyfriend . . ."

"Really," Karen was all ears, "so what happens to this girl now? Does she go on being jealous or what?"

"Well, she will do if she doesn't meet a good fairy soon. I told Oriel she shouldn't have done it, 'specially not so near Christmas, but it's her favourite trick and she can't resist showing off . . ."

"What are you then, a good or bad fairy?" Karen smiled, half-serious, half-joking, waiting for the reply.

"Me? Oh, I'm good. Well at the moment I am." A mischievous grin curled the pouting lips, "you want to make the most of me though, I may not be good for long!"

"So, if this jealous girl met you she'd be all right would she?"

"Oh yes, I'd help her see things the way they really are. Take all that nasty green jealousy dust out of her eyes. I think that humans are very silly to let something as small as a bad fairy upset them. But then, we fairies are pretty clever." The little girl patted her dress and shoved her slipping garland once more.

Karen laughed. This kid, wherever she came from, was really cute—even if she did tell a few prize fibs.

As she smiled, Karen realised that it was the first time she'd felt happy for a week. The coldness had gone from inside her and suddenly she noticed the beautiful frosty winter's day and the tingle of Christmas in the air.

"Hey," she wrapped her scarf round her neck, "I'm getting cold sitting here and you must be suffering from double-pneumonia by by now, so come on, I'll walk you home and we can . . ."

She turned round but the log beside her was empty. The child had disappeared, suddenly and soundlessly. Karen walked quickly into the wood but could see nothing except—what was that?—it looked like a flash of silvery spider-web gossamer darting between the trees. And was it her imagination, or did she hear the trees whisper, "Happy Christmas"?

Karen shrugged. That child, she couldn't really have been a-a-a **fairy**? Silly. Impossible. But . . . Anyway, she'd gone now and it was time for Karen to go too. Time for her to go back to home . . . and Steve.

As I said, Christmas Eve is a nice day for most fairies. And it can be pretty nice for humans, too, especially if they happen to meet a good fairy who's doing over-time . . .

GREAT

Glitterin' GARY!

Life's all go for superstar Gary Glitter... but when he does get a spot of spare time he doesn't sit about — he gets stuck in to one of his many hobbies!

Leave a horse within a couple of miles of Gary and he'll hunt it out and be galloping over the horizon as quick as a flash... and if he's not spending his spare time ridin' horse-back then he's on a jet plane to the sun, the sea... and hours of swimming! If he's only got a day or two to spare then there's nothing he loves better than to wander round the old junk shops searching out old curiosities 'n' goodies — oh, and he always takes his camera with him on these jaunts 'cos photography's one of his favourite hobbies too! So next time you're window shoppin' keep an eye out for a glitter in the crowd... it could be our Gary!

GARY
GLITTER

BEAUTY FOR ALL SEASONS
Making Faces All

Just as fashion changes with the seasons — so should your face. Pick the lighter, cooler colours for the spring and summer months and the deeper warm colours for the winter.

WINTER

Winter means cosying-up with lots of warm colours and that's why blushers are so important at this time. It also means lots of reddy lipsticks to give your smile a lovely glow. And for the eyes? Darker shades of blue, mauve, green, any colour you like — just so long as it's shiny!

SPRING

When Spring comes along your make-up should change, with a lighter foundation and a more tawny blusher to start with. For the eyes, stick to the shiny shadows but in lighter colours — or the same colours applied sparingly (if you can't afford new ones). Change to a brown mascara to give your eyes a more natural summery look. Lips should be much paler — with lots of gloss and just a little colour. And at this time of year, it's a good idea to give your skin an extra special cleanse. It can make all the difference to your skin.

DONNY OSMOND

TOGETHER!

To make sure you're looking top-to-toe perfect you've just gotta get those accessories together. An outfit just doesn't look complete without those little extras and whether it's a small piece of jewellery or a fun hat they're a must! So grab a load of these ideas and get your looks into shape!

Have you got your hat yet? There are so many different styles about that there's just got to be one for you and whether it's a woolly pull-on for the winter, or a cotton sun hat for the summer they're really fun and look great. And if you can get some scarves and mitts to match — wow, what an outfit!

Believe it or not, tights are very important, too. They can do a lot towards making or breaking that outfit. The choice of colours is so enormous now, that if you want to match 'em up with that pretty dress, you're bound to find a pair to fit the bill — just look around!

Choose pastel colours for the summer and for a dramatic effect in the winter, how about stunning seams or even fishnet tights? And don't forget, no ugly ladders please! Nothing spoils the effect of a pretty outfit more — so if you haven't got a decent pair, dash out and buy some more or wear trousers instead!

You could class shoes as a necessity — well they are but they're also an accessory. Not many people can afford more than say two pairs at a time, so you've got to match them with all your other togs (unless you happen to have a lot of lime green clothes a pair of lime green shoes aren't really going to be worn very often — now are they!)

So stick to basic colours like black, brown and navy — you'll have no trouble matching up then — and, don't forget, remember your feet aren't going to appreciate it much if you spend a day shopping in elegant high-heeled shoes so treat 'em well, eh!

Handbags need choosing with care too — they don't necessarily have to match your shoes, just so long as they blend in well with everything else.

Jewellery is perhaps one of the most important accessories around and you don't have to spend a fort-une to start your collection either. There are plenty of super bangles, big beady chokers, pretty pin-ons, rings and ear-rings which you can pick up really cheaply — and they make all the difference to any outfit.

Finally, belts have always been in the shops, but they've only recently become a very important accessory, so make sure you've got yours — whether it's thick 'n' chunky for denims, or narrow.

Now you're really lookin' together!

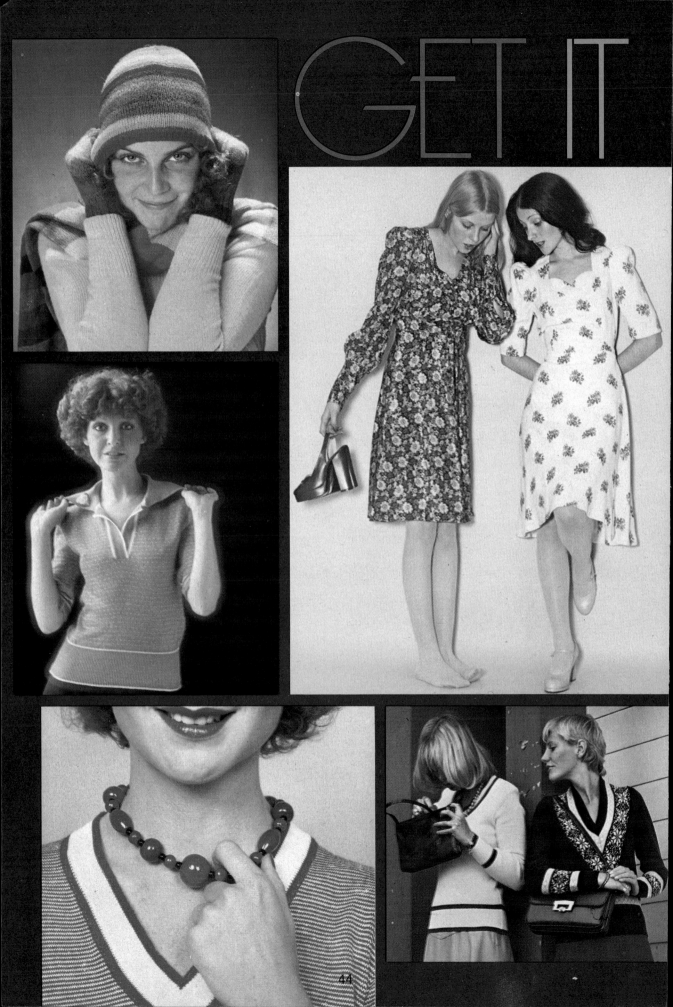

SUMMER

Summer is the best time for any skin, 'cos assuming you get some sun on it, nothing can make it clearer, brighter or healthier. So make the most of it. Forget about foundation for the time being, and just use lots of moisturiser, with a touch of eye-shadow, lots of mascara and some shiny lip gloss.

AUTUMN

By the time Autumn comes around your skin should be in lovely condition from all those sunny days, so just use a bare foundation to give you a touch of colour. Stick to the fairly pale shades eye-wise, but add some colour to your cheeks and lips and look as golden as the autumn leaves.

Kindle a Flame'

Bring a do-it-yourself light into your life . . . and get yourself equipped with a candle-making kit!

Though it's not really difficult, it's quite technical — what with wax, stearin, wicks, perfumes, dyes, thermometers and moulds — it's great fun if you're the budding scientist of your gang!

Seriously tho', this way you can make lots of beautiful candles — on the cheap — and once you get the knack, there's nothing stopping you displaying your wares at Church Bazaars or whatever!

Start off fairly simply until you find your feet. But then you can really go to town and there's no knowing where this creative bent could lead!

All you need, to begin your dazzling career as a candle-maker, are: a kitchen with a couple of saucepans (Mum's consent is rather essential here — and we'd grab the oldest saucepans you can find!), a sugar thermometer (that's one with high temperatures on it. Ask your mum, granny or cookery mistress) — and of course, a candle-making kit.

The kit we used cost approx. £3. You may think that's expensive but, believe it or not, it made all the candles in our pic! It came from Candle Makers Supplies, 4 Beaconsfield Terrace Road, London W14 0PP. Send them 5p for a wall chart full of information and details of prices.

There're easy-to-follow instructions for melting the wax and making it up into candles. Where your ingenuity comes in is finding things to use as moulds. Yoghourt cartons, glass jars, cardboard tubes, etc. — any of these'll do.

You can buy rubber moulds too, so that your candles come out with a carved surface. Trouble is, they're so gorgeous you won't want to burn them!

Or, if you fancy having a go on a smaller scale to begin with, you could try whipping up some wax!

Whip Wax is just like . . . meringue. You add water, and mix. Then use it to decorate plain candles — you can even put it in an icing tube and pipe out wax flowers!

Candle Makers Supplies make a Whip Wax kit, too — so write to them for details, as above.

Altogether, we're quite taken up with the idea of making candles. So c'mon, we bet you're just burning to get going!

Sharon was worried. It was very late and her Mum and Dad would be going potty. But they mustn't know where she had been. Not since Dad had put his foot down and forbidden her to see Dave any more . . .

She remembered the scene at home when Dad had found out from a friend who she was dating: "I have heard about his family," ranted Dad. "Rough lot. Always in trouble with the police. I am telling you, Sharon, you must never see this boy again. He is bad like the rest of his family. Now promise you won't see him again."

Sharon hadn't wanted to promise. Dad had kept on and on at her, in the end she had promised. Promises are easy to break — when the very next day she had seen Dave on her way to work.

She meant to tell him that she would never see him again. It just wouldn't come. The words stuck in her mouth. Instead she arranged to meet him. Go to his house. Meet his parents. They welcomed her. They seemed such nice people his Mum and Dad.

"Stay for coffee," said Dave's Mum. And they had all sat there talking for ages. Suddenly Sharon had noticed the time. What could she tell her parents as she hurried home?

★ ★ ★

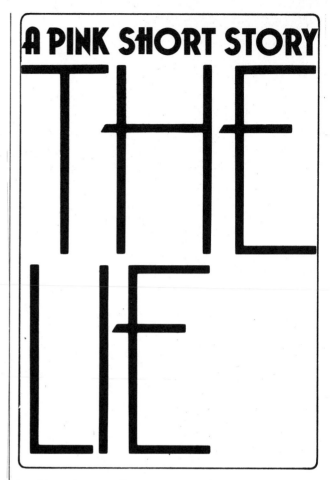

THE LIE

She was walking down a badly lit street by some shops. Suddenly the sound of breaking glass — a bell ringing. Running footsteps coming towards her. A young man dressed in black. He was running her way. Quickly Sharon hid in a shop doorway. The sound of a siren coming up the street. Police!

The running figure stopped, Sharon pressed herself further back in the shopway. It was dark, but her eyes got used to it and she could see vaguely. There was a shuffling sound and Sharon heard heavy breathing, panting, near her. She turned her head. The thief had chosen the same shopway to hide in! She could see his face quite clearly. He hadn't seen her.

The siren was getting closer and closer. A car flashed by, its blue light glowing into the shopway. Sharon's blood ran cold, the man had spotted her. He knew she was there, and that she had seen him. What would he do?

"I — I'll scream," said Karen, forcing the words from her mouth. "You won't stand a chance." The young man seemed to hesitate, then suddenly he dashed from the doorway.

"You tell the police," he said over his shoulder, "and I'll find you. I know you." Then he was gone.

Karen stood there, her knees trembling. She felt faint. But then the siren was coming back towards her again. The police would be searching this street again. They mustn't find her. Her parents would find out where she had been, they would guess. What could she do?

Quickly and quietly, Sharon hurried from the shop doorway and down the street. Glancing back she could hear the siren, but the police car had not come in sight. Sharon hurried on. The road became lighter and the headlights turned into the street. The siren had stopped now, but the car was coming nearer. The police must have seen her!

Suddenly the police car was stopping beside her. The window was wound down and a voice called, "Wait a moment Miss, you may be able to help us."

Managing to smile, Sharon went over to the car. "How can I help?" she asked sweetly.

"There was a robbery at the jeweller's shop in this street tonight," said the Police Officer, getting out of his car. "We were wondering if you saw anything. There was a tip-off that a shop would be done tonight. We were waiting. But by the wrong shop. Did you see anything?"

Sharon knew she would have to lie, if only so save herself from Dad's fury.

"No, no, nothing," said Sharon. But her eyes betrayed the lie.

"Are you *sure*, Miss?", said the officer, a doubting look on his face. "There is no need to be frightened. You can speak up. No-one will hurt you."

Sharon was frightened. Somehow she realised that the policeman didn't believe her. But she couldn't tell him the truth. She couldn't. "I have just left my Saturday job," she lied again. "Overtime, you know. It is late, I must be going home. My parents will be worried."

Then quick as a flash, Sharon turned and ran. A narrow alley was nearby, the car could not follow. She was so quick, that the Police Officer was taken by surprise, and before he had even started his pursuit, Sharon was sprinting halfway down the alley.

In the distance Sharon heard the siren start up again. But she took more alleys and soon she realised that the Police would not find her that night.

Mum and Dad were worried. But when Sharon explained about the overtime, they believed her.

After her experiences of the evening, Sharon couldn't get to sleep. She lay there tossing and turning. Remembering that young man's face, the accusing look of the policeman, the chase, lying to her parents.

Perhaps if she broke off with Dave. The police would

never find her, she could stay indoors. Work overtime. Keep out of the way until everything blew over . . .

It was Sunday the next day, no work, no school, Sharon decided to go right round to Dave's house — tell him she never wanted to see him again. She knew it would be the hardest thing she ever had to do, but it was for the best.

Dave was surprised to see her that morning.

"What is it, Sharon?" he asked, seeing the look on her face. "What is the matter?"

"I won't stay long," said Sharon, keeping her voice as steady as she could. "I just came round to say I don't want to see you ever again. I have heard what you are really like, and I just don't want to see you again. Ever!"

Dave's dad came out. Sharon hadn't realised her voice had gone a bit hysterical.

"What do you mean?" he asked. "What is Dave really like? Explain yourself, young lady."

Sharon broke down sobbing. Telling them everything.

She had just stopped, when the doorbell went. It was the police. One of them was the same Officer who had questioned Sharon the night before. Sharon's legs started to shake, the room started to spin — everything was going dark . . .

Sharon came to, lying on the sofa in Dave's front room. His Mum and Dad were there, so was the officer.

"Don't worry," Dave was saying. "It is all right. They have come to find my brother."

"Your brother?" gasped Sharon. "I didn't know you had one."

Dave looked upset. His dad butted in, "Yes, Roger, the eldest and the black sheep of the family. Always in trouble. Last night he broke into a jeweller's shop. But there is a witness."

Sharon's heart leapt to her mouth. Dad would find out, now. She was the witness. She knew it.

"Yes, an old man was putting out his milk bottles when he saw Roger race by. It was dark, but he is positive it was Roger. But that doesn't explain why you ran away last night, young lady."

Sharon explained that she had seen the young man, about the promise she had made to her parents because of what her dad had said about Dave's family. A promise she had broken . . .

"Come on", said the policeman. "Your father has got everything wrong. Dave is well-known to us, he is a police cadet. Training to be one of us. It isn't his fault his brother is a bad one."

Dad wasn't at all pleased to see Sharon turn up in a police car. But when everything was explained, he admitted he had been wrong.

"I shouldn't listen to idle gossip," he said. "I should have trusted my daughter to choose her own boyfriend."

Sharon sighed with relief. It was over. She needn't lie any more. And who knows, one day, she could even become a policeman's wife!

If there's one thing that's almost guaranteed to break up a boy 'n' girl relationship it's that old 'n' familiar story of parent trouble . . .
'Cos when parents start complainin' that it's all gettin' too serious, it's just not possible to please them *and* yourself *any more — and you've just got to take sides.*
Well, that's what happened to Anna and Pete. So read their story — written from both sides — and see what you think about their broken romance.

Whose side

Anna's story

"His attitude's changed towards me . . . now I've got to take second place."

To tell the truth, the whole thing was a huge shock to me . . . the last thing I ever expected to happen. It just goes to show how wrong you can be about people . . . even people you thought you knew really well.

Pete 'n' me have known each other for over a year — and we've been goin' out together now for nearly ten months. But, somehow I just know that it's not gonna last much longer . . . at least, not unless he's prepared to completely change his attitude towards me. And, somehow, I can't see that happenin'.

He's made it quite clear how he feels about me. And that can be summed up easily enough — I've got to be prepared to take second place.

It wasn't always like that. At the beginning, I was his Number One — there was no doubt about that. I reckon in those first few months just about everything we did we did together. We were inseparables. Our mates even used to kid us about it, but we didn't care. That was the way we wanted to be. Then Pete began to change.

At first, he didn't actually say anything to me, but I could tell there was somethin' up — the way he suddenly started lookin' at his watch when we were out together and makin' up excuses about how he'd have to get back early 'cos he had homework to do.

And when I'd 'phone him up, instead of soundin' all pleased to hear my voice like he used to, he'd act all strange, like he couldn't wait to get off the line quick enough.

Of course, it was all bound to come out into the open sooner or later — and eventually it did. But when he told me that it was all to do with his mum 'n' dad I could hardly believe my ears!

"His folks seem to think he's too young to go steady. But that's rubbish — Pete's sixteen!"

I suppose I knew from the start that they weren't too keen on me — especially his mum — but it had never really bothered me. Pete was all I cared about. Anyway, I knew it was nothin' personal on their part, 'cos they didn't even know me.

It was just that they didn't approve of their beloved son goin' steady. They thought he was too young or somethin' to start gettin' serious about a girl — any girl. Which was rubbish, of course. I mean, Pete was sixteen!

Well, apparently, over the months they'd been gettin' more 'n' more upset about our relationship. His mum was sayin' that we went out together too much and stayed out too late (which wasn't even true, 'cos I always had to be home by ten and it only takes Pete twenty minutes to walk back from my place).

According to her, too, I was keeping Pete off his schoolwork. In other words, I was a bad influence and it had to be stopped!

Well, if it had been up to me I would have just told her to get lost. She was just bein' silly 'n' selfish anyway.

But, of course, it wasn't up to me — it was up to Pete. And this is where I got the biggest shock of my life . . . because Pete took his mother's side!

Of course, he tried to kid on that he wasn't, but when a fella starts saying that maybe we shouldn't go out together quite so often any more and maybe it would be a good idea if I stopped 'phonin' him at home when his folks were home — just because that's what his mum wants — whose side would you reckon he was on? Well, I reckoned he certainly wasn't on mine. And I told him so.

"It was the biggest shock of my life when he took his parents' side against me . . ."

That was about three weeks ago. Of course, we had a terrible row. I was in tears and I think Pete was pretty close himself. But he refused to give way.

He positively insisted that to 'cool things down a bit' (his words!) was the only way we were gonna make it work out in the end.

But I told him he was just makin' excuses. It was obvious that he cared a lot more about his mum than he cared about me.

My feelings didn't even come into it! And I said I thought he was nothin' but a Mummy's boy and that I didn't want to have any more to do with him.

But I didn't really mean it — and Pete knew I didn't. What I really wanted was for him to change his mind and for things to be like they used to be. But Pete said they couldn't. It had to be his way.

Well, of course, things haven't been the same between us since then. In fact, they've been pretty bad. We

are you on?

still see each other — occasionally. But I refuse to go out every time he asks me. So sometimes I say 'No, I have homework to do' or something — even tho' it's not true. I refuse to let him think he can use me when he feels like it.

It makes me pretty sad, though. I mean I really do miss him. I wish I knew what was going to happen now . . . If only things could be like they used to be.

Pete's story

I don't really know where to start . . . Y'see, the whole thing started brewin' up long before Anna really knew about it. I suppose my big mistake was that I tried to keep it from her for as long as I could. I suppose I knew how she would react. She's pretty possessive about me.

"Every evenin' when I got home Mum'd be waitin' for me all long-faced and angry . . ."

Anyway, right from the start, as soon as they realised that I was serious about her, my folks began objectin' to me goin' out with Anna. Well, you know how parents are — especially mothers — they still like to think of you as little kids even when you're perfectly grown up. They felt I wasn't 'ready' for a serious

relationship, that I should just concentrate on my schoolwork for the time being.

Well, I suppose in a way I could see their point. I mean they've sacrificed a lot to let me stay on at school, and they're really dead set on me goin' to University. And, naturally, they were scared that Anna might prove to be too much of a distraction for me. My dad said as much.

Of course, I tried to persuade them that that wasn't gonna happen (and I meant it, too — I'm as serious about makin' a career for myself as they are!), that Anna wasn't gonna interfere with anything. In fact, if they'd only known it, she gave me an incentive to work even harder. But they would never have believed that!

At first, they kinda seemed to accept what I said. When I think back now, I suppose, really they were just hopin' that Anna and I would just blow over in a couple of months and then they'd have nothin' more to worry about. But, of course, that wasn't what happened at all. And when Mum began to see that we really were serious after all, she really started to put the heat on.

Every evening after we'd been together, she'd be at home waitin' for me, all long-faced 'n' angry, demandin' to know where we'd been, what we'd been doin' and reminding me that the house wasn't a hotel the way I seemed to think it was. It got to be a really tacky situation.

You know, I didn't want to have to start seein' less of Anna. Heavens, she's the most important thing in the world to me! But I just couldn't go on with things the way they were at home. So, I tried to figure out what the best thing was to do . . . and it seemed to me there was really only one solution. I decided to tell Anna.

Well, I didn't exactly expect her to be over the moon about what I'd decided, but I didn't expect her to be so unreasonable about it either. After all, all I was askin' was that we should try and cool things down a bit — for a while anyway. See a bit less of each other — that was all. And it wasn't exactly because I wanted it. It was just because, quite honestly, I couldn't see any other way.

"Somehow I just couldn't do what Anna said and tell them to get lost . . ."

Of course, like Anna said, I could have just told my parents to get lost and carried on regardless. But, somehow, I couldn't do that. In a way, I could understand what they were on about, tho' they were exaggeratin' a bit, of course. Besides, the atmosphere was gettin' so bad at home that it was pretty well almost unbearable. Much more of Mum's constant inquisitions and Dad's criticisms and I reckon I would've looped the loop.

Another thing was this. Y'see, I know my folks pretty well. They're a bit old-fashioned and all that, but on the whole they're not really all that bad. And I was pretty sure that if I could just let them see that they had nothin' to worry about and kinda get them on my side, sooner or later (and probably sooner) they'd come round and start seein' things my way for a change. It was just a matter of time.

"There's only one person whose side I want to be on — and that's Anna's . . . but she refuses to see my side."

I told Anna that. That it would just be for a few weeks — just long enough to get things back to normal at home, really. Then I thought I would talk them round to meeting Anna — maybe have her round for dinner some Sunday or somethin'. And once they got to know her I just knew everything would be all right.

But Anna refused to see it that way. It was like she thought I was tryin' to get rid of her or somethin' — the exact opposite to the truth! She accused me of takin' my folks' side against her, and I know that tho' it may look a bit like that it's not really like that at all.

Really, there's only one person whose side I want to be on — and that's Anna's. Only she refuses to see things from my point of view.

I hardly ever see her now. Every time I 'phone she comes out with these phoney excuses about bein' busy with other things. I only hope we can get together again, tho'. I'd never get over it if we didn't . . .

54

56

57

HAVE YOU GOT BOUNCE?

. . Well, you know what we mean — are you the kinda girl who's always full of get up 'n' go, the first to suggest merrily, 'Who's for tennis?', or are you a peaceful soul, happy to tag along with life's sweet way — as long as it's not too strenuous . . . ? Read on and find out!

1 It's Friday night — disco time again! Your mates'll be down there bouncin' around to all the latest hits. How do you dance the night away?
a. You dance excitedly to the records you like a lot — but only if you can feel the 'beat'.
b. You wait till a dishy fella asks you — and then preferably when it's a slow, smoochy record playin'!
c. You dance to everything 'cos you love it, only taking a quick breather to sip your Coke before you start boppin' again?

2 You're spending the weekend with your country cousin. She's a real horse fiend and suggests you go riding with her, tho' you've never tried before. Do you:
a. Agree to go willingly, altho' (inside) the thought of it gives you the colly-wobbles.
b. Of course you go! — you've always wanted to ride horse-back — and have a

BOINNNG!!

great time bouncin' up 'n' down on your Neddy's back.

c. Decide to go to the stables to stroke the horses, but you won't ride 'cos you weren't prepared and haven't got the right kinda gear.

3 It's your birthday and your boyfriend buys you tickets for both of you to go to a top superstar concert. At the last minute he rings up to say the concert's cancelled. How d'you react ?

a. You burst into tears, bitterly disappointed — after all it was meant to be your birthday treat.

b. You tell your fella it doesn't matter — but he can tell from the tone of your voice that it does.

c. It's not the end of the world — so you put on your special birthday dress just the same and suggest you go and see a movie instead.

4 While on holiday Mum 'n' Dad take the family on an afternoon sailing trip. Mid-way the weather takes a turn for the worst. Soon it's gettin' a bit rocky 'n' rainy. Do you :

a. Join everyone else and take cover below, thinking what a bore this trip turned out to be.

b. Pull on your sou'wester and sit rooted, enjoying the salty breeze — after all, isn't this what sailing's all about ?

c. Dash under cover, turning gradually greener 'n' greener, wonderin' if you'll ever set foot on land again ?

5 One mid-March morning you wake up, the sun's shining warm thru' your bedroom window, the birds're singing . . . Spring's definitely in the air ! How d'you start the day ?

a. Jump up, throw your clothes on and do a few energetic jigs around the garden before breakfast.

b. Sit up in bed enjoying the warm sunshine, thinkin' of all the things you're gonna do now Spring's here.

c. You don't — that sun's really makin' you squint — so you pull the covers over your head, turn over and go back to sleep again.

6 You meet a smashin new fella at the disco and, to your delight, he asks to see you again. It doesn't take you long, however, to discover that your latest heart-throb's the original football fanatic soon he asks you to go and watch him play one Sunday afternoon. There's just one snag — it's pelting down with rain and frost-bitten fingers weather. What's your reaction ?

a. You make the excuse that you've gotta wash your hair . . . and you've got masses of homework to do.

b. You go along and after standing wrapped in woollies from head-to-foot till half-time you decide you can't stand it any more and retire to his dad's car and watch the rest of the match from there.

c. You don your football-watchin' gear, get out your rattle and watch your heart-throb's every move.

1. a)5 b)0 c)10.
2. a)5 b)10 c)0.
3. a)0 b)5 c)10.
4. a)5 b)10 c)0.
5. a)10 b)5 c)0.
6. a)0 b)5 c)10.

HOW DID YOU DO?

0—15
Well, it can never be said that you throw yourself whole-heartedly into the joyous things in life . . . in fact, the way you're goin' on, you must have a pretty miserable time of it. Try to look on the bright side of things a bit more, Life's what you make it, you know — so try 'n' find a bit more energy to get involved in some fun activity — if you turn over a new leaf now, some of those mates of yours might just give you another chance to join in with them, instead of dismissing you for the down-on-the-ground, stick-in-the-mud you are !

20—35
You've got some bouncy, fun ways about you but you're not on the whole consistent. One minute you're up in the clouds, dreamin' about what you *could* achieve, the next you're taking things on their face value — and that way you'll never get the most out of life ! Be a bit more adventurous, have the courage of your convictions, instead of being put off by the slightest draw-back, and you'll soon come up smilin' !

40—60
Golly — seems like you're the kinda person we could do with jollying around in the Pink office . . . you'll be able to cope with our daily catastrophes if anyone can ! There's never a dull minute in your life, is there ? You've always got a smile on your face, always ready to come bouncin' back — even if things do go wrong . . . which they won't do for long with you around ! Well done — you're one of those lucky people who's always got the Umph ! to get the most out of a situation, and life — you'll go far. Good for you !

61

Your future! That's what this is all about! Whether you get to work on a super magazine like Pink or as a busy secretary/nurse/ hairdresser, your career — your future — is something you'll have to start thinking about soon!
And having to make the decision on what you're going to do can be the hardest one of all. So if you're not sure what sort of job is just right for you, we take a look at some of the many around, give you an idea what they're all about, and, most importantly tell you what qualifications you'll need . . .
Whether you want to be a scientist, a model, an archaeologist, a teacher, they're all here! So read on . . .

'SOCIAL' CAREERS

If you're the friendly type who likes helping people why not consider a career in *Social Work?* There is a wide choice of jobs in this field — from working with very small children as a nursery nurse, to community work, or working in your local hospital.

For most careers in this section you do need a minimum number of O-levels (and in some cases A-levels) but this is something your teacher would advise you on. If you wanted to go in for Nursery Nursing for example, you would need only four or less O-levels/CSE exams to qualify. You would then do a period of training depending on how far in

nursing you wanted to go.

The best openings for social work are with your local authority or hospital who would be only too glad to help you if you wrote to them (or perhaps your Mum would?). Or you could write to the Central Council for Education and Training in Social Work, at Clifton House, Euston Road, London NW1, for information.

CLERICAL WORK

Secretary: Being a secretary doesn't mean you're going to sit in a typing pool for the rest of your life — tho' that is where a lot of secretaries start to get a bit of experience for their next, big, job! Secretarial work can be fun and very interesting and lead to all sorts of opportunities, if you're prepared to work for them!
Qualifications: You do need a few O-levels/CSEs, including English and maths. You can either take shorthand, typing, arithmetic/ accounts and office practice at school or go on and take them at college. The length of the course depends on the college and your preferences.

Once you're a qualified secretary you can get a job anywhere — working in a newspaper's offices, a modelling agency, a big, busy factory, a college, a solicitor's office . . .
Bank Clerk: Working in a bank would be too much temptation for our Jamie, we can't even trust him with the *tea* money! But we know you could be trusted — and banking is an interesting career, too.
Qualifications: You need five or less O-levels or CSEs including English and maths (of course!). Once you've joined a bank they will send you on a part-time course at a technical college for the Institute of Bankers' diploma.

Here again is another career

with lots of opportunities — if you're prepared to work for them! We haven't heard of a woman bank manager yet — but there's always a first time! The Institute of Bankers at 10 Lombard Street, London EC3, will give you more information.
Civil Service: offers all kinds of clerical work. As a *junior clerk* you would need a minimum of two O-levels/CSEs including English or English language.

You can soon move up in the Civil Service to a clerical assistant and later clerical officer, which includes the Diplomatic Service, and has always sounded fascinating, a bit like under-cover

THINGS TO COME...

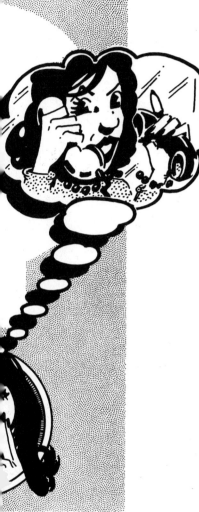

dealing with very old books — but there is a lot of routine work involved, like cataloguing.

Qualifications: It is possible to work as a library assistant and work your way up — but only so far, as all responsible positions need qualified people. So if you can, it is best to get three O-levels including English language, and two A-levels required to do a two-year full-time course. You can go on the course immediately after you leave school, or a year or two after you've been working in a library to make sure you really like it.

Archaeology: Train to do this and you could find yourself digging up another Pharoah's tomb in Egypt! Sounds a bit far fetched we know, but it *is* possible! The training is pretty tough for this profession though . . .

Qualifications: You need at least five GCEs, two of which must be A-level; one of which should be chemistry. You should also be able to do metal-working and/or pottery.

There are some alternative qualifications but check these with your teacher.

NURSING/SCIENCES

Nursing: There are so many different aspects of nursing it is best for you to decide first what particular line you will take and then discuss the qualifications you need. Usually tho', the minimum age for training is 18 so it might not be a bad idea for you to perhaps work voluntarily at your local hospital during the school holidays as a nursing auxiliary to see if you like the work.
The Nursing and Hospital Careers Information Centre at 121/123 Edgware Road, London W2, will give you further information.

Doctor: Training to be a doctor is a longish process and here again,

this is something you should discuss with your careers teacher in detail.

Lab Technician: A really interesting and enjoyable career if you like sciences. You can either be a medical lab technician or work in a science lab.

Qualifications: For ordinary lab technician work you need 4/5 O-levels including two sciences and English, and for a medical lab technician four O-levels, two sciences, one English and one other. Your best way into this job is to join a laboratory and then take a two year part-time course at a local college to become properly qualified.

THE SO-CALLED 'GLAMOROUS' JOBS:

People always think *Journalism* is a glamorous job — but it's not, it's jolly hard work involving quite a bit of drudgery sometimes! (Mind you none of us would change for *anything!*)

Qualifications: A minimum of five O-levels is needed, and A-level is recommended. Usually you join a local paper and do six months' probation (to see if you really like the job), followed by three years' indenture (traineeship). You also do two eight-week block-release courses during this time for the National Council for the Training of Journalists certificate, at the end of your three years.

Alternatively, you can get 100wpm shorthand, chat up the editor of your local paper — and take it from there!

Modelling: No qualifications needed really, you've just got to have the right figure and looks. Some girls go to a modelling school but a lot of the top models were just discovered (Twiggy for example). It's all a matter of luck!

Air Hostess: What a lovely way to see the world but it's not all jet-

agent/James Bond sort of stuff to us!

The Civil Service Commission at Alencon Link, Basingstoke, Hampshire, will send you any information you want.

TEACHING, ETC.

To be a teacher you need a minimum of five O-levels and one or more A-levels wherever possible. Usually you decide what you want to teach, what age children, and then go to a Teacher Training College for a three year course.

Librarian: Just the job if you're a real little book-worm! It can be fascinating tho', specially if you're

YOUR CAREER

setting about!

Qualifications: a good standard of education to O-level is needed.

No minimum specified but it is useful to have English language, geography, maths, domestic science and at least *one* foreign language. Usually you join one of the air lines and do a six/eight week course at a training centre — then go on your first test flight. Minimum age of 19 (but this varies with the air lines, so why not write to them for more details?).

Beautician: No qualifications specified but it is an idea to have at least three O-levels. Usual method of training is to (a) do a course at a beauticians' school (mainly in London), or (b) write to the major beauty firms, like Max Factor or Elizabeth Arden, enquiring about their training schemes.

Acting: A pretty tough career if you want to make it to the top — but if you've got the 'bug' and the talent, you won't let that stop you!

Qualifications: O- and A-levels not specifically required, but they are useful, especially in English.

Training is usually a three-year full-time course at a drama school, or you might be very, very lucky and join a local rep. and take it from there. Acting can also lead to stage management, production, even films . . .

As we said, it is a difficult career to succeed in so it might be as well to have a secretarial training to fall back on during lean times . . . !

ART AND DESIGN:

This offers a wide, wide field of careers, from graphic design to furniture and industrial design, fashion, textile and interior design, not to mention display work, jewellery, photography, and set design. This is something to really discuss with your careers teacher, and why not write to the National Council for Diplomas in Art and Design at 16 Park Crescent, London W.1.

for information.

Fashion Buying: O- and A-levels are not necessary for this career, but again, useful. Usual method of training is to join a large store and then train through one of their schemes. You will begin as a junior or under buyer and maybe work in all departments of the store to gain first-hand knowledge of the business. Write to one of the large stores like Debenhams or John Lewis for details.

ANIMALS:

Veterinary Surgeon: If you're an animal lover this is the obvious career for you — but there are other openings.

Qualifications: A minimum of five O-levels, including a science, and A-levels and further education are essential. Write to the Royal College of Veterinary Surgeons at 32 Belgrave Square, London SW1 for further information.

Zoo-keeping: Now this sounds really interesting and something quite different too!

Qualifications: No qualifications are specified but it is obvious that a few, including a science, would be very useful. Usual training is by joining a zoo and then going on part-time/block release courses. The Zoological Society of London at Regents Park, London NW1 will give you more info.

We know this is only the tip of the iceberg as far as careers available are concerned, but we've kinda run out of space! Just remember that, tho' it's sometimes hard to stick at your schoolwork, however hard you work, whatever you achieve, is all for *your* own good in the end.

There'll come a time when you'll be enjoying your job, whichever career you choose, and you'll thank yourself for trying for that extra O- or A-level! Remember, too to take the opportunity of learning shorthand and typing whilst you're at school, if you can fit it in . . . it's incredible how useful this can be for you in *all* fields later on.

Anyway, hope these ideas have given you food for thought! Good luck! .

The way to his HEART

...is through his stomach. And it applies to the stars in your life as well as the boy down the road. So here's the way to a few star hearts...

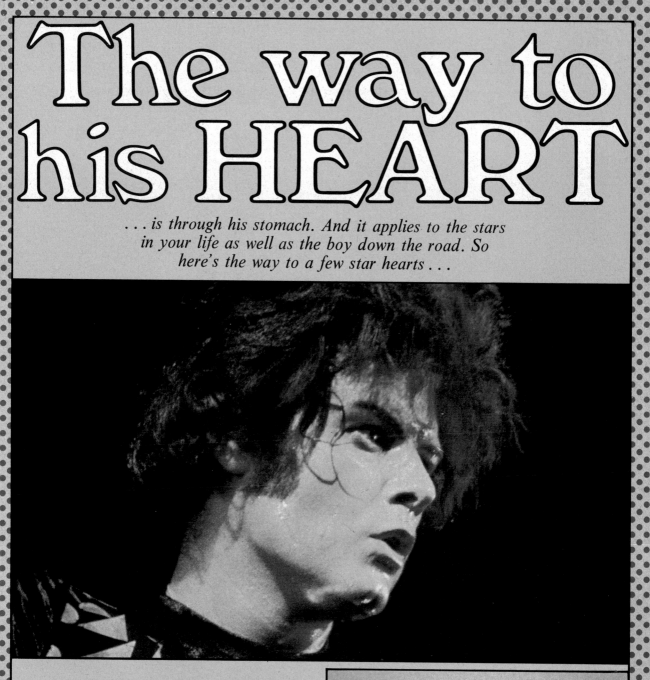

GOOD OL' HOME COOKIN'

Gary Glitter's a country lad at heart — so for him we made this country casserole. It serves four, so you can always invite a couple of the Glitter Band along as well!
You'll need: 4 chicken portions, 2 onions (chopped), $\frac{1}{4}$ lb. (100 gm.) mushrooms (sliced), 2 tomatoes (sliced), 1 lb. (450 gm.) new potatoes (sliced — use tinned ones if you're feelin' lazy!), 1 can condensed cream of chicken soup (use undiluted), 1 pinch mixed herbs.
Just put all the ingredients in a casserole dish in the oven (350°F) for about an hour, or until the chicken's tender. We're sure Gary'll smell it cookin' long before then — he won't be able to resist the tempting aroma!

The way to his HEART

FLIPPED OVER 'EM!

We reckon Rod Stewart'd really flip over these pancakes! First, mix together 1 egg, 4 oz. (100grm.) flour, and $\frac{1}{4}$ (140 ml.) pint milk, and leave to stand for an hour. Heat some oil in a pan — now cook your eight pancakes! 'N' keep 'em warm while you make this delicious sweet 'n' sour filling . . . 1 can pineapple; 1 oz. (28 gm.) sugar; 2 tbs tomato sauce; 1 large carrot, grated; 1 tbs cornflour; 2 tbs vinegar; 4 oz. (120 gm.) peeled prawns. Drain pineapple and, in a saucepan, add water to juice to make $\frac{1}{4}$ pint. Add sugar, tomato sauce and carrot; boil; cover and simmer for 5 mins. Blend cornflour and vinegar and stir into saucepan; simmer for 2 mins Then add prawns. Pour a little filling on to each pancake. Mmmm! Watch Rod come runnin'!

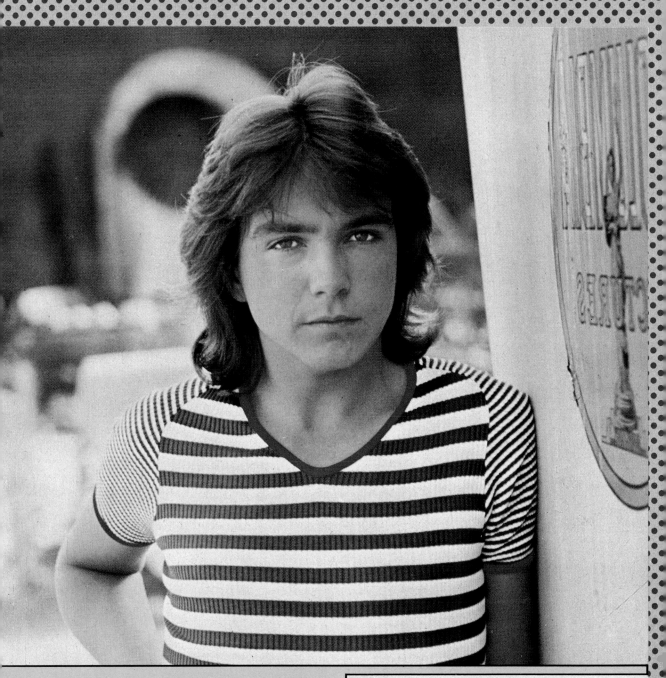

ALL FULL UP

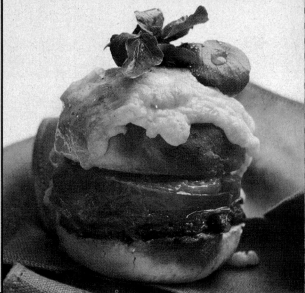

Despite all his fame and glamour, David Cassidy's just like us at heart when it comes to a good old nosh-up and, for a special feast, he goes a bundle on real, home-made cheesy beefburgers!
So why not treat yourself — and David! Take 2 bread buns, 2 onions, chopped and fried, 2 frozen beefburgers, 2 large slices cheddar cheese. Fry the beefburgers and lightly toast the bun. Arrange a burger and onions inside each bun. Now put a slice of cheese over the top of each — and toast 'em for two minutes. That wasn't so very difficult now, was it? And we're sure that David would be beggin' for seconds!
Well, didn't you enjoy cooking for your favourite stars? We bet you did — and so did they!

So let's start with the most important part of your beauty routine — skin care.

Cleansers and toners can be quite expensive so why not try Rosewater and Witchazel instead ? (you can buy them both from most chemists).

After you've washed your face, cleanse your skin with a dob of cotton wool soaked in Rosewater — it smells fantastic and leaves your skin feeling smooth and fresh.

Next, substitute your usual toner or astringent for Witchazel, which is excellent for tightening up those pores and lessening the risk of blackheads.

And what about those flushed, rosy faces ? They needn't be. Ease too much red this way . . . just take a slice of cucumber and stroke the insides of it on your cheeks and leave it to dry . . . yes, really!

As for that crowning glory of yours, here's where Rosewater comes in handy again . . . Use it as a final rinse when washing — it really will give your hair a super sheen and leave it smelling of roses too !

Another great rinse for your hair is vinegar, so ask Mum if you can have a little. And if you want a substitute for setting lotion there's nothing better for making your hair glossy and bouncing than a cupful o' Dad's beer — let's hope he'll oblige.

BUDGET BEAUTY

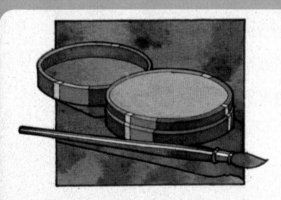

Eye-wise, using brushes to put on your shadow is much easier than the ol' finger, but why not buy a paint brush instead ? — It costs a lot less than the cosmetic kind and does the job just as well. As the hair is much softer and more supple, you'll find nothing better for applying eyeliner with. You can get a really fine, line.

And to get tired eyes really sparkling, grate a raw potato and put it between two layers of gauze or three-ply tissue. Now take forty winks with a piece of this on each eye, leave 'em there for about fifteen minutes and relax! Cucumber is great for this, too but it's more likely that there are potatoes in the house!

Blushers can be an extra luxury you can't afford, but since using one is so important to give your face shape and colour don't despair. Just dig out that red lipstick — great if you wear one — and put a couple of dots on your cheeks, then using your finger smooth it in.

And don't forget — never throw old lipsticks away — by using a lip-brush (or a paint brush of course) you can easily use more than one lipstick to get a different colour — in fact you should never throw any make-up away — you never know when it's going to be useful. Store it in plastic bags for a rainy day.

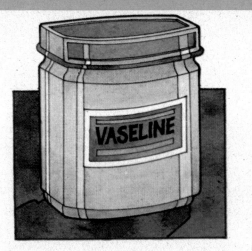

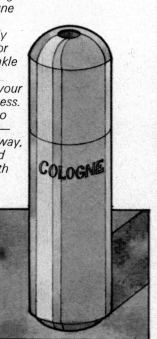

Money doesn't always stretch as far as you would like it to and if after buying a lipstick you can't afford a lip gloss try using Vaseline — a jar will last for ages and ages and looks just as good as a real lip gloss. And for those winter months it's a great protector against chapped lips — so always keep it on you.

And while the attention's on your mouth, how about those teeth? Try brushing them occasionally with salt — it may not taste too good — but it does wonders to whiten them — really!

When bath time comes along it's always nice to pamper yourself — so why not buy one of those huge, cheap bottles of cologne (from Woolworth's or Boots) — they're really economical and last for ages — and then sprinkle a little into your bath water — it will make your skin tingle with freshness. Or if you just happen to have eaten an orange — don't throw the skin away, just score the skins and then put 'em in the bath while the taps are running — another great skin tonic!

The herbs you'll find in Mum's kitchen are full of beautifying goodness too! Just put some in a muslin bag, tie this to your bath taps while the water's running–that's it!

When that lolly seems a little short there's no need to give up all those beauty routines ... 'cos there's some really cheap ways to make yourself as beautiful as ever, and you might even find some of them at home this minute! Don't believe us? Then follow a few of our budget beauty recipes and look just as lovely ... the penny-saving way!

And finally what about face masks? Home-made ones are just as good and much more fun than the packet ones.

Eggs can make a great mask; whip up the white of an egg, then if there's any honey around add a teaspoon of that to the egg, spread it on your face, leave if for 10 minutes then wash off.

Tomatoes are also great for toning the skin and a tomato mask will help dry up a greasy skin and close ugly open pores.

A squashy one that no-one wants to eat is a great recipe for this: Mash the tomato — with the pips removed, mix with 1 teaspoon of milk or ½ a teaspoon of olive oil. Spread the mixture on your face, leave for 10 minutes then rinse off and you should be left with a smooth silky-looking skin.

If your skin is rough and dry try mixing two tablespoons of oatmeal or porridge oats with enough milk to make a soft paste (and if you've got that Rosewater handy add a drop or two — it makes it even nicer). Leave it on your skin for 15 minutes and just see what a difference it makes!

So now you're set — make yours a budget beauty!

SPOTLIGHT ON YOU

Wotta lovely lot of readers Pink's got! It's nice when you get a chance to model for us in the magazine — like our happy crowd below! Thought it'd be nice to take another look at when Pink put the spotlight on you!

Lyn and Silvana were two lovely sisters we used for a fashion session — and as soon as we sat them in front of the camera we just couldn't believe it! Born models if we'd ever met any! "We enjoyed every minute of it!" they said.

Donna was runner-up in our Pink model competition. She's got lovely long dark hair and deep brown eyes. We were so impressed by her that we asked her to model for a four-part booklet called How To Be The Girl You've Always Wanted To Be.

"I was so excited I just couldn't believe it," said Donna. She comes from Lancashire so we brought her down to London for two days spending one day shooting lots and lots of beauty pictures and the next day shooting fashion.

"I don't really know which I preferred, and I certainly didn't realise what hard work it can be! Even so I loved every minute of it."

We must admit we did have to work hard during those two days, but since Donna wants to be a model when she leaves school the experience was invaluable, "It hasn't put me off at all," said Donna.

Debbie *(Below)* is someone else who's been seen in the mag — on the cover quite a few times too. With her fresh face and dark brown eyes, she was a natural cover girl.

CONTINUED ON PAGE 72

Although Donna is very serious about becoming a model she's carrying on with her studies first. "I know modelling isn't an easy thing to do, so I'm making sure I've got something to fall back on." A very wise lady!

Debbie hasn't any ambition to become a model. "It's not that I didn't enjoy working for Pink, I really did. And I must admit it is flattering to be seen on a cover of such a great mag. None of my friends would believe me — until I showed them! I think they were quite envious!"

71

SPOTLIGHT ON YOU

CONTINUED FROM PAGE 71

Here's another Debbie! This time a lovely blonde who modelled for Pink beauty. "It was absolutely fantastic — just like a dream come true." Remember super Susan the lovely winner of our Model Competition? She certainly deserves to make it in the modelling world and we're sure she will!

Mandy was probably one of our youngest and first readers to model for us, "I was very nervous, but it was great fun." And here's our last lovely blonde, Debbie with her fantastic smile. She was yet another super model reader!

How many times have you regretted something you said or did which you know hurt someone you were fond of? Often enough, I expect, to know that apologising, saying you're sorry, can be one of the most difficult things in the world.

A thoughtless word here, a heedless action there, can cause a lot more sorrow than you ever dreamt of, making someone else unhappy.

And the only way to make them feel better — and you look them straight in the eye again without feeling guilty — is to say you're sorry . . . and mean it.

It's no good saying, "I'm sorry" to your mum because you've hit your rotten little brother again, because he was annoying you — again — because you don't really mean it. Your mum knows that too, y'know, she's not daft! Chances are she went thru' the same with her equally rotten little brother (now your dishy uncle) too!

So she knows how you feel — but that's no excuse for going round bashing your kid brother!

STOP 'N' THINK!

Really, the best thing is to try and avoid a situation whenever possible where you might end up hurting someone (verbally I mean, not the kid brother bashin' kinda thing!). You can't always avoid them I know (you'd have to be super-human to do that!), but you can try.

F'rinstance, if there's an argument among your class mates and one girl's coming off worse than the others and you're dying to join in with something you know is a bit spiteful against her, bite your tongue rather than say it. Think how rotten she'll feel when you say it in front of everyone — and how mean you'll feel too, by hurting her like that in front of the class.

Even if she is a bit unpopular with the rest of the class, that doesn't give you licence to be horrible to her, does it? She's more than likely feeling pretty miserable about it already and

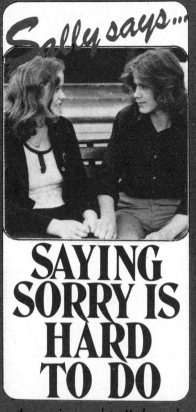

Sally says...

SAYING SORRY IS HARD TO DO

A row is good to "clear the air" as they say. But often in a fit of temper we say things we don't mean and regret afterwards. It's then we have to "eat humble pie" and say we're sorry — and that's often the hardest part of all . . .

you don't really want to add to her unhappiness, do you?

Just stop and think for a moment how you'd feel if the boot was on the other foot and it was *you* they were against. Wouldn't like it, would you?

If you are nasty to her tho', afterwards be brave and say you're sorry to her — in front of the others. You will make her feel better and perhaps your class mates will realise they've been a bit unfair to her.

Later you could catch her up on the way home, explain that you really meant what you said and maybe you could be friends from now on. You'll make her school life a lot happier, y'know — honest.

THE FAMILY WAY . . .

More often than not we find ourselves apologising after a row because it is when we're angry we say things we don't mean . . . arguments with the family happen all too easily, often because we are all so close and fond of each other. They affect the whole family too, even if the row is just between you and your sister, because you probably won't be speaking to each other either. Very awkward at meal times! So everyone's glad when you make up.

Making up with your fella after you've had a 'lover's tiff' is always nice — 'spect he'll buy you a box of chocs or something into the bargain. But don't fall out with him too often just to make up again — he'll either get wise to your little game or won't be able to stand the strain of endless tiffs!

Sometimes we have to say we're sorry for things that aren't our fault. Like being late to meet a friend at the cinema and missing the beginning of the film — all because the bus was late.

Then we really do mean it because her, and your, evening has been spoilt and neither of you were to blame.

The impression people have of you, and your friendship, can depend a lot on how you treat people, and being able to accept that you were wrong goes a long way. Someone who is stubborn and full of self-importance doesn't win friends easily.

So it's as well to know how to apologise genuinely. Perhaps a fail-safe way is to think how you would like someone to say sorry to you — and know that you could believe them.

The genuine person will always go further than someone who is insincere — saying sorry or whatever right, left and centre without really meaning it, 'cos sooner or later she'll be found out . . .

But remember, the prevention is always better than the cure . . .

TRIM UP TO SLIM UP

Even if you don't need to lose a few extra pounds, exercise is a must. It's the only way to keep your figure trim and fit. So do a few of these stretchers and get yourself into shape. But remember — don't overdo it at first otherwise you'll ache all over!

BELOW for tummies and thighs, lie flat on the floor with your knees bent and slowly raise your body off the floor, slowly go back to your lying position and repeat. ABOVE For slim arms . . . Slowly rotate elbows in a circular motion.

LEFT: For tummies and thighs. Sit on the floor with legs outstretched, slightly apart. Stretch arms out to the side and swing them round to touch opposite toe, i.e., left hand to right toe. Then use opposite arm and leg.

TOP LEFT: For chin and neck rotate head first one way then the other. TOP RIGHT: For tummies. Holding a towel over your head, bend to the floor, knees straight. BOTTOM LEFT: For bottoms, when you're in the bath roll from side to side. BOTTOM RIGHT: For thighs. Lie in the bath, bend legs and stretch to ceiling, bend back, repeat.

For tummy and back thighs. With legs straight bend over and touch your toes. No cheating now, those legs must be straight.

ABBREVIATIONS: K. = Knit;
P. = Purl; st. = stitch; tog. =
together; alt. = alternate; rep. =
repeat; patt. = pattern; in. =
inches; M.1 = make 1 stitch by
picking up horizontal loop lying
before next stitch and working into
back of it; C.6 = slip next three
stitches on cable needle to front of
work, K.3 then K.3 from
cable needle.

HAT AND SCARF WITH CABLE DETAIL

Materials: Of Patons Doublet,
Hat: 2(50 gram) balls.
Scarf: 7(50 gram) balls.
No. 7 needles and No. 4 needles.
MEASUREMENTS: Hat to fit
average head. Scarf 60" long,
excluding fringe, 7½" wide, approx.
TENSION: 8 sts. and 9½ rows to 2",
measured over stocking stitch on
No. 4 needles.

HAT

With No. 7 needles, cast on
83 sts. and work in rib as
follows:— 1st row — (Right
side), K.1, * P.1, K.1, rep.
* to end. 2nd row — P.1, *
K.1, P.1, rep. from * to end.
Rep. last 2 rows until Hat
measures 1½ in., ending with
1st row. Next row — Rib 9,
(M.1, rib 2, M.1, rib 19)
3 times, M.1, rib 2, M.1, rib 9
(91 sts.).
Change to No. 4 needles and
work in patt. as follows:—
1st row — (Right side), K.
2nd row — K.8, (P.6, K.17)
3 times, P.6, K.8. 3rd row —
K. 4th row — As 2nd row.
5th row — K.
6th row — As 2nd row.
7th row — K.8, (C.6, K.17)
3 times, C.6, K.8. 8th row —
As 2nd row. 9th row — K.
10th row — As 2nd row. 11th
row — K. 12th row — As 2nd
row. These 12 rows form
patt.
Continue in patt. until Hat
measures 5 in., ending with
right side facing for next
row.
Keeping continuity of cable
panels, shape as follows:—
1st row — K.3, K.2 tog., K.3,
(patt. 6, K.2, K.2 tog., K.3, K.2
tog., K.3) 3 times, patt 6, K.3,
K.2 tog., K.3 (80 sts.).
2nd and every alt. row — In
patt. 3rd row — K.3, K.2 tog.,
K.2, (patt. 6, K.2, K.2 tog.,
K.2, K.2 tog., K.2, K.2 tog.,
K.2) 3 times, patt. 6, K.2, K.2
tog., K.3 (69 sts.).
5th row — K.2, K.2 tog., K.2,
(patt. 6, K.2, K.2 tog., K.3, K.2
tog., K.2) 3 times, patt 6,
K.2, K.2 tog., K.2 (61 sts.).
7th row — K.2, K.2 tog., K.1,
(patt. 6, K.1, K.2 tog., K.3,
K.2 tog., K.1) 3 times, patt. 6,
K.1, K.2 tog., K.2 (53 sts.).
9th row — K.1, K.2 tog., K.1,
(patt. 6, K.1, K.2 tog., K.1, K.2
tog., K.1) 3 times, patt. 6,
K.1, K.2 tog., K.1 (45 sts.).
11th row — K.1, K.2 tog.,
(patt. 6, K.2 tog., K.1, K.2
tog.) 3 times, patt. 6, K.2
tog., K.1 (37 sts.).

13th row — K.2 tog., (patt. 6,
K.3 tog.) 3 times, patt. 6, K.2
tog. (29 sts.). 15th row —
K.1, * (K.2 tog.) 3 times, K.1,
rep. from * to end (17 sts.).
17th row — K.1, (K.3 tog.,
K.1) 4 times (9 sts.).
Break yarn, thread through
remaining sts., draw up
tightly and fasten off
securely. Join back seam
with a flat seam.

SCARF

With No. 4 needles, cast on
30 sts. and work 7 rows
garter stitch (every row K.).
Next row — K.14, M.1, K.2,
M.1, K.14 (32 sts.).
Work in patt. as follows:—
1st row — (Wrong side),
K.13, P.6, K.13. 2nd row — K.
3rd row — As 1st row. 8th
row — K.13, C.6, K.13.
9th row — As 1st row. 10th
row — K. 11th row — As 1st
row. 12th row — K.
Rep. last 12 rows until Scarf
measures approx. 59 in.,
ending with 3rd row. Next
row — K.13, K.2 tog., K.2,
K.2 tog., K.13 (30 sts.).
Work 7 rows garter stitch. Cast off.

Cut remaining yarn into 10 in.
lengths and taking 3 strands
together each time, knot
along short edges to form a
fringe. Trim fringes.

ABBREVIATIONS: K. = knit;
P. = purl; st. = stitch; rep. =
repeat; in. = inches; tog. =
together; sl. = slip; p.s.s.o. = pass
slip stitch over; patt. = pattern;
d.c. = double crochet.

SUN DRESS

MATERIALS: 4 5,5 (50 gram) balls
or Paton Limelight Crepe — knits as
4 ply.
No. 10 needles. 3.00 mm (11)
crochet hook. ⅓ yard or
round elastic.
MEASUREMENTS: To fit 32, 34,
36 in. bust.
Wearing length 32, 32, 32 in.
TENSION: 7 sts. and 9 rows to
1 in. slightly stretched.

FRONT

** With No. 10 needles, cast
on 163[181,199] sts.
1st row — P.4, K.2, * P.7, K.2,
rep. from * to last 4 sts., P.4.
2nd row — K.4, P.2, * K.7, P.2,
rep. from * to last 4 sts., K.4.
Rep. 1st and 2nd rows until
work measures 5½ in., ending
with 1st row.
1st dec. row — K.2, K.2 tog., *
P.2, K.5, K.2 tog., rep. from *
to last 6 sts., P.2, K.4
(145[161,177] sts.). Next row
— P.4, K.2, * P.6, K.2, rep.
from * to last 3 sts., P.3.
Next row — K.3, P.2, * K.6,
P.2, rep. from * to last 4 sts.,
K.4. Rep. last 2 rows until
work measures 10½ in.,
ending with wrong side
facing.
2nd dec. row — K.3, * P.2,
sl.1, K.1, p.s.s.o., K.2
(127[141,155] sts.). Next row
— P.3, K.2, * P.5, K.2, rep.
from * to last 3 sts., P.3.
Next row — K.3, P.2, * K.5,
P.2, rep. from * to last 3 sts.,
K.3. Rep. last 2 rows until
work measures 13½ in.,
ending with wrong side
facing.
3rd dec. row — K.1, K.2 tog.,
* P.2, K.3, K.2 tog., rep. from
* to last 5 sts., P.2, K.3

Even the world's worst knitter could have a go at these! And whether it's a beefeater for a baby brother or sister or a snappy little sun dress for you it's easy once you get going! — And if you do get stuck perhaps Mum will give you a hand!

(109[121,133] sts.). Next row — K.2, P.2, * K.4, P.2, rep. from * to last 3 sts., P.3. Rep. last 2 rows until work measures 16½ in., ending with wrong side facing.
4th dec. row — K.2, * P.2, sl.1, K.1, p.s.s.o., K.2, rep. from * to last 5 sts., P.2, sl.1, K.1, p.s.s.o., K.1 (91[101,111] sts.).
Next row — P.2, * K.2, P.3, rep. from * to last 4 sts., K.2, P.2 Next row — K.2, * P.2, K.3, rep. from * to last 4 sts., P.2, K.2. Rep. last 2 rows until work measures 21 in., ending with wrong side facing. * *
Place a marker at each end of last row to indicate top of side seam.
Next row — Work 45[50,55] sts., K. into front and back of next st., work to end.
Next row — Work 46[51,56] sts., turn leaving remaining sts. on spare needle.
Continue on these sts. as follows:— Work 25 rows.
Next row — P.2, * K.2, P.2 tog., P.1, rep. from * to last 4 sts., K.2, P.2 (38[42,46] sts.).
Continue as follows:—
1st row — K.2, * P.2, K.2, rep. from * to end. 2nd row — P.2, * K.2, P.2, rep. from * to end.

Rep. 1st and 2nd rows 4 times more, then 1st row again.
Next row — P.2 tog., K.2 tog., rep. from * to end (19[21,23] sts.).
Next row — K.1, * P.1, K.1, rep. from * to end. Cast off in patt.
Rejoin yarn to remaining sts. and complete to match first side.
BACK
Work as for Front from * * to * *. Cast off in patt.
MAKE UP
Press each piece lightly with a cool iron and dry cloth. Sew side seams. Knot one end of elastic. With right side of work facing hold elastic at cast-off edge of Back with knot at side seam. Work a row of d.c. along cast-off edge, working into each st. and taking the yarn over the elastic to form casing. Fasten off.
Cut elastic to required length and knot other end. Sew knots securely at side seams. Make 2 twisted cords using 5 strands of yarn 90 in. long. Knot ends and trim. Attach a cord to cast-off edge at each side of front as follows:—
With right side of work facing hold cord at cast-off edge. Now work a row of d.c. along this edge, working into each st. and taking the yarn over the cord to form casing. Fasten off.
Press seams lightly.

ABBREVIATIONS: ch. = chain; d.c. = double crochet; tr. = treble; h.tr. = half treble; d.tr. = double treble; s.s. = slip stitch; st. = stitch; in. = inches.

FLOWERY PULL-ON
MATERIALS: Patons Kismet, 1 (50 gram) ball.
Odmet of Kismet or 4 ply yarn in Snow White.
No. 5.50 mm (5) and No. 3.50 mm (9) crochet hooks.
MEASUREMENTS: to fit average head.
TENSION: 3½ h. tr. measures 1 in width using double yarn and double No. 5.50 hook.

CROWN
With No. 5.50 hook and yarn double, make 5 ch. and join in a ring with s.s.
1st round — 2 ch., into centre of ring work 13 h.tr., s.s. in 2nd of 2 ch. (14 sts.).
2nd round — 2 ch., 1 h.tr. into same st. as s.s., (1 h.tr. in next st., 2 h.tr. in following st.) 6 times, 1 h.tr. in last st., s.s. in 2nd of 2 ch.
3rd round — 2 ch., 1 h.tr. in same st. as s.s., (1 h.tr. in each of next 2 sts., 2 h.tr. in following st.) 6 times, 1 h.tr. in each of last 2 sts., s.s. in 2nd of 2 ch.
4th round — 2 ch., 1 h.tr. in same st. as s.s., (1 h.tr. in each of next 3 sts., 2 h.tr. in following st.) 6 times, 1 h.tr. in each of last 3 sts., s.s. in 2nd of 2 ch.
Continue in this way increasing 7 sts. on every round until there are 70 sts. Work 2 rounds straight. Fasten off.

SIDE PIECE
With No. 5.50 hook and yarn double, make 31 ch.
1st row — 1 h.tr. in 7th ch. from hook, (2 ch., miss 2 ch., 1 h.tr. in next ch.) 8 times.
2nd row — 4 ch., miss first h.tr. and 2 ch., 1 h.tr. in next h.tr., (2 ch., miss 2 ch., 1 h.tr. in next h.tr.) 7 times, 2 ch., miss 2 ch., 1 h.tr. in 4th of 7 ch.
3rd row — As 2nd row, ending last h.tr. in 2nd of 4 ch. Repeat the last row until fabric fits round head when very slightly stretched. Fasten off.
TO MAKE UP
Do not press.
Stitch one long edge of side piece to Crown.
Join the 2 short ends of Side Piece and gather up tightly, fastening securely.
FLOWERS
With Contrast and No. 3.50 hook, make 5 ch. and join in a ring with s.s.
1st round — 2 ch., (* into ring work 1 tr, 1 d.tr., 3 ch., 1 d.c. in top of last tr, into ring work 1 d.tr, 1 tr, * 1 d.c.) 4 times, work from * to *, s.s. in top of 2 ch. Fasten off.
Make 10 more Flowers, 5 each in Contrast and Main Shade. Stitch Flowers in a cluster to point where Turban is gathered.

77

YOUR NEW YEAR STAR SPINNER

Your horoscope sign can take a very important part in your life and your future. And we've been busy picking out the exciting things your stars have in store for you in '76 ...

AQUARIUS
(January 20 — February 18)

This is the age of Aquarius, so they say — and it sure looks as if this is your year!

Altho' your serious nature sometimes takes the upper hand, enjoying life'll be second nature to you and, socially, the months'll whizz by before you know it! You'll still keep your head work-wise, 'tho', which means a lot can be achieved at school or with the hobby you take an interest in.

Friends will feature strongly in your life — one in particular. This will be the year when romance takes a new turn for you. An important and happy relationship is in store.
MAGIC MOMENTS: February and the latter part of August will be rich in memorable occasions.
MONEY: This will be the year when your attitude to money is more responsible — you'll have more to handle!
LUCKY COLOUR: Turquoise.

PISCES
(February 19 — March 20)

Your very sensitive and mystical nature flourishes in calm and peaceful surroundings early this year. You come into your own within your crowd of friends and win a new and sincere respect from them. Perhaps a new romance will also happen when you least expect it — whatever, one way or another, you'll feel more confident so that, later in the year, you branch out a little, socially, and have a good time! This could develop in the future, too.

Altogether, it's a year of new beginnings, so make the best of it. There're plenty of opportunities just there for the taking.
MAGIC MOMENTS: June is your month. You feel that everything's great just then.
MONEY: You need to feel more independent, so try to get some money of your own together.
LUCKY COLOUR: Sea-green.

ARIES (March 21 — April 20)

Your outgoing and direct personality could take you a long way this year — but don't make any rash decisions that could spoil your chances. Think carefully about matters — even tho' they may not seem that important. Early on in the year you'll set yourself a goal — maybe a romantic one — and don't give up 'cos towards late Spring you'll begin to see all that hard work pay off!
MAGIC MOMENTS: February and April — they could be ones that you'll remember for the rest of your life!
MONEY: Go easy on the spending. There's no telling when that rainy day will come!
LUCKY COLOUR: Red.

TAURUS (April 21 — May 20)

The new year starts for you in a gay social whirl — and you're very popular. 'Course, you'll have to expect a bit of a lull — maybe around May, but life'll soon pick up again! Don't be afraid to strike a close friendship with one person in particular — those other friends'll still be around!

In the Autumn, there's a strong chance of a long-term romance developing slowly —but whatever you do don't try to rush it, or you could risk losing a deep and loving relationship.
MAGIC MOMENTS: You'll have to wait a bit. It's your turn to shine in May and June.
MONEY: It comes and goes this year — try not to let it slip through your fingers.
LUCKY COLOUR: Indigo blue.

GEMINI (May 21 — June 20)

Your busy and changeable nature has been moving round in circles for a while, hasn't it? But early on in the year you'll find more than enough to keep you happy and interested in all the happenings. Could be a fantastic new hobby will catch

your interest — a possibility of travel or a really super holiday looks hopeful.
You'll be happy to find too, by August and September, that a couple of close friends are more important to you than lots of casual acquaintances.
MAGIC MOMENTS: Early on ... February and March are gonna be your highspots.
MONEY: Be prepared to work for it!
LUCKY COLOUR : Yellow.

CANCER (June 21 — July 21)

This'll certainly be a memorable year for you!
You begin to come out of your shell at last, Miss Cancer! But be careful not to let your sensitive emotions run away with you — 'cos you could be deeply hurt — especially where boyfirends are concerned. Just don't get too involved until you know you're on safe ground!
Summer should be a happy and successful time and long-distance travel is indicated.
MAGIC MOMENTS: One special weekend in late May, or June, has you up in the clouds!
MONEY: A chance to earn some on the side — perhaps a Saturday job — and this could develop later.
LUCKY COLOUR: Violet.

LEO (July 22 — August 21)

Tread softly at the beginning of the year. You're a born trend-setter, but if you're not careful you'll risk upsetting some of your quieter chums. Try to go along with the crowd a bit more and fall in with their plans.
You can do well without making quite so much noise about it, you know! You should try too, to get on with people of all ages. We can't all be young ravers — and you'll be grateful for advice around Autumn.
MAGIC MOMENTS: Springtime has you all a-flutter, and March could be extra special.
MONEY: You'll find people surprisingly generous, especially around birthday time. But money isn't everything!
LUCKY COLOUR: Orange.

VIRGO (August 22 — September 22)

Mind you don't get stuck in a dull routine 'specially in the Summer. Your tidy mind can easily get rather fussy! If you're not careful you'll forget how to let yourself go and have fun!
Don't forget to keep in touch with all your friends — get out and do things, anything, just so as you've got something different to talk about! Expect the beginning of a deep and long-lasting friendship.
MAGIC MOMENTS: There're two high-spots for you this year. In late January, and again in May or June.
MONEY: It's there to spend, you know. Careful you don't get too cautious with it!
LUCKY COLOUR: Brown.

LIBRA (September 23 — October 22)

You're pretty steady and reliable by nature, but this year could see you going through a few exciting changes. Possibly because of a change of scene or meeting a whole new set of friends. Either way, you'll let yourself go a lot more.
The year starts off looking decidedly rosy — you think you've got it made! Be pre-pared for some quiet times in between the fun.
Careful, tho' — in March or April your castles in the air could come tumblin' down. But that lull won't last for long — around June you really start to flower — and romance is starred.
MAGIC MOMENTS: Your fun-time will be in the Summer — around mid-July.
MONEY: You have a financial goal to meet around holiday-time.
LUCKY COLOUR: Blue.

SCORPIO (October 23 — November 21)

You're bouncing full of beans, but careful you don't tire yourself out at an early age! Make sure

you use all that energy constructively, and there'll be no end to your achievements this year.
A jolly social time is indicated ... Maybe you'll join a youth club group or something similar — either way, it'll be a busy year!
MAGIC MOMENTS: In April you feel just great, and suddenly everything seems to be going just right.
MONEY: You'll certainly try to stretch it a long way.
LUCKY COLOUR: Dark red.

SAGITTARIUS (November 22—December 20)

True to your sign, you're full of high ideals — and this is the year to try to fufill them. Others may try to put you off your goals — but the choice is yours — so stick to 'em! Don't get involved in things which go against your nature — especially at school — just because you think they'll make you more popular. People will respect you more for being just you!
MAGIC MOMENTS: You'll shine in the Autumn. September should be a great month for you.
MONEY: You're very generous. But just be careful that people don't take too much advantage of you.
LUCKY COLOUR: Purple.

CAPRICORN (December 21 — January 19)

This'll really be the year when Miss Capricorn finds her true self. At present, there is a tendency to hide your real, deep-down feelings — but all this will change ...
In the Spring you'll be touched by romance — much to your surprise. And you'll find yourself at your happiest — it'll be so new and refreshing!
There'll be lots of things going on — suddenly you'll have loads to choose from.
MAGIC MOMENTS: March and June are lucky for you. There's love in the air!
MONEY: You'll be better off by the end of the year. The stars are shining on you!
LUCKY COLOUR: Emerald green.

Are you WITH IT

Fashion and beauty looks change all the time—but do they affect the way you live? Are you the kinda girl who likes to be seen wearing the very latest style no matter how outrageous it is? Do you know how to adapt a fashion look to suit YOU, personally? Or don't you care much about the way you look . . . ?

Find out if fashion and beauty play an important part in your life, by doing our fantastic 'with-it' quiz . . . !

1. Which are the most important to you:
a. The way you look.
b. Doing well at school.
c. Having a good time?

2. When you read your favourite mag (and its got to be PINK!) what do you turn to first:
a. Your fave strip story.
b. The fashion/beauty pages.
c. The pop poster?

3. You go to see an exciting movie, very reminiscent of the 30's. What do you notice most:
a. The beautiful clothes, and hairstyles.
b. The gorgeous hero.
c. The horrid bits (you goulish creature you!)?

4, A new fashion look is in for autumn. You can't afford to buy it straight away, so do you:
a. Save like mad till you've got enough pennies gathered together.
b. Don't bother about it at all—in fact you've hardly noticed that fashion's changed lately(!)
c. Get out your sewing machine, adapt an old pattern, and make your own just as good as those you've seen in the shops and at a quarter the price!

5. What do you think is the most important beauty asset:
a. A good skin.
b. Healthy, shining, well cut hair.
c. A good figure?

6. Carrying on from question five— to keep yourself looking and feeling good do you:
a. Watch what you eat, try to eat healthy, fresh things whenever possible and get enough sleep each night.
b. You don't bother at all and carry on munching thru' those choc bars.
c. You try—sometimes?

7. Who is the woman you'd most like to be:
a. Beautiful and gauche like model/actress/singer Twiggy.
b. Stunning and sensational like Bianca Jagger.
c. A legend in your own right a la Greta Garbo?

OR WITHOUT IT?

4. a (5), b (0), c (10).
5. a (10), b (5), c (0).
6. a (10), b (0), c (5).
7. a (10), b (5), c (0).
8. a (10), b (0), c (5).
9. a (5), b (0), c (10).

Your Rating:

60—90: You've got your wits about you, there's no doubt about that! You're very aware about what's going on, read fashion and beauty mags avidly and follow trends without question. No inhibitions or doubts for you! But sometimes you can overdo it—remember that fashion looks should reflect you, the kinda person you are, so don't be just a walking fashion model, use clothes to their best advantage, revealing the nice, bubbly person you are! Full marks tho' for caring so much 'bout the way you look!

30—55: You're on the right track—but need a bit more courage sometimes, don't you! You're sensible about the way you look tho', know what really suits you, and that's what matters after all—personality is often reflected in the way we look. But don't shy of putting on a show once in a while—you can get away with it if you're brave enough (and you are really, aren't you?!).

0—25: Oh dear, all our fashion 'n' beauty pages are wasted on you . . . But we're not giving up by any means! There are lots of things to be interested in we know, but now's a very important time when you should be caring about your skin, your figure etc.—it'll show later on. You can start on your basic wardrobe too, finding out what styles and colours suit you. So c'mon, don't miss out on all the nice things that make it worthwhile being a 1976 lady —trendy lady at that!

ø. You like the new looks yes, but always end up with the same old blue/green eyeshadow, pink lipstick look?

9. Last year it was the chunky layered look for autumn/winter, did you:
a. Wear it—immediately.
b. Think twice about it—it mightn't suit you.
c. Knit youself an extra long scarf, matching pull-on gloves and cardi— now there's initiative for you!?

8. New make-up looks are always coming on the market, do you:
a. Always try them out—in the safety of your own bedroom, of course!—and adapt them to suit you.
b. You don't bother much about make up for yourself.

SCORE:

1. a (10), b (5), c (0).
2. a (0), b (10), c (5).
3. a (10), b (5), c (0).

THE DOLL

Tracy groaned when her mother mentioned Humphrey Griggs — he wasn't the sort of boy she had in mind for her party. But two other guests were to give Tracy an even greater shock — and they hadn't been invited . . .

OH, DAD! **NOT** AT MY CHRISTMAS PARTY? WE'RE NOT KIDS ANY LONGER!

WHAT DOES THAT MATTER? THERE'S NOTHING LIKE A LITTLE LIVE ENTERTAINMENT TO MAKE THINGS GO WITH A SWING — NO MATTER HOW OLD THE GUESTS ARE, TRACY!

84

85

CLOWNIN' AROUND

Suiting each other musically isn't the only
ingredient that makes a good group . . . bein' really
good mates is another very important factor!
Slade are all the best of friends, and they make sure
that they enjoy themselves together, however
frantically busy they are . . . !

*You have to be pretty good mates to be
able to spend your working life together
and then meet up in your spare time . . . but
that's what Dave, Noddy, Don and Jim do.*

*The lads are all practical jokers, 'specially
Noddy!*

*One day, f'rinstance Noddy felt
particularly mischievous so he decided to
catch Dave out. Y'see, Dave's always
nagging Noddy 'cos he's always late for
things, and the last to get to rehearsals!
So when Dave was out of the room
just before they were
about to nip out
to a practice
Noddy glued
Dave's
boots to
the
floor!*

*Of course Dave rushed in, went to pick his
boots up to put 'em on . . . and couldn't!*

*"Oh c'mon or we'll be late," yelled
Noddy. The other two were fallin' about
with laughter . . . and so did Dave when he
discovered why he couldn't pick 'em up!*

SLADE

A STITCH IN

If you're handy with a needle then take a look at this—and if you're not—still take a look, 'cos if you can make your own clothes it really is cheaper than buying 'em.
And not only that, it's a great feeling to know that what you're wearing was made by your own fair hands. It just takes a little time and a little patience. So come on get out those needles and pins and make it easy.

For our Stitch in Time we decided to make five different items that all mix 'n match. And not only that, we didn't just stick to plain fabrics. Mixing and matching patterned fabrics does take a bit more thinking about but the effect is far more exciting. To mix and match patterns you really need to choose the same fabric, varying only the pattern and colour. With the five different pieces of clothing we made there are three completely different looks. All of the clothes are really easy to make — and you can still match the clothes you already have to make even more alternative outfits. And this is how we did it!

TIME........

The trousers, jacket, top and skirt are all from Butterick pattern no. 4029. The dress is made from Butterick pattern no. 4030. We made the skirt, jacket and trousers in one of the fantastic Mary Quant fabrics which she has designed for ICI. The fabric, believe it or not, is Crimplene (at last someone has updated it) and we think the result is pretty good. You can wash it, squash it, sit on it and it still won't crease — so it really is quite remarkable. It's 60" wide and costs about £2-£5, depending on the type you choose!

CONTINUED ON NEXT PAGE

91

A STITCH IN TIME......

CONTINUED FROM PAGE 91

The blouse is made in another Quant fabric this time Celestial Crepe. (All these fabrics are made under the name Ipatra.)
The tie-fronted dress is made in a Suncrest fabric which is a Polyester-jersey mix and the colour is Pimento.
The yardage for the clothes in 60" fabric is:
skirt: $1\frac{1}{4}$ yds; Jacket: $1\frac{1}{8}$ yds plus 1 yd for trim; trousers: $1\frac{3}{4}$ yds; blouse: $1\frac{1}{8}$ yds; dress: $3\frac{1}{4}$ yds.
For details of the stockists of the Mary Quant fabrics, please write to ICI Fibres, Box 800, 565-577 Kingston Road, Raynes Park, London, S.W.20.

SPARE TIME STARS.....

Being a superstar is pretty much a full-time occupation, y'know! What with all that travelling, performing and busy hiring it must be tough to find even a minute to spare. But some top popsters manage it! We know you're all dying to find out what the stars do in their spare time; so we've grabbed some gorgeous piccies to give you an inside view of what some super special stars get up to in their off-stage hours.

First off is Alvin Stardust, caught here showering his spare-time affection on his kitten. And can you blame her for enjoying it? And here's Paul McCartney, retiring off-stage at his Scottish farm (with Linda and the children, of course) and enjoying the fresh air.

SEE NEXT PAGE

Elton John and Rod Stewart are just spartan lads at heart, really. They still get their kicks from playing football . . . we really love their get-ups, too! Here they're snapped with Mike Parkinson.
Barry Blue's a different kettle of fish, though. In his spare time he collects interesting junk — like this giant ice-cream cone. Coo-ooo-ool!

SPARE TIME STARS....

CONTINUED FROM PAGE 93

Super drummin' lad Cozy Powell's quite speedy in his spare time, 'cos he's really at home on the racing circuits. His garland in the piccy shows that he's quite a star there, too — as well as on the pop scene!

Here's our Cozy again, looking very serious about it as he has last words with Noel Edmunds before leaping in — to leap off!

Another of your fave stars who gets away from the heat of the stage and plunges behind the wheel of a racing car — is John Rossall (Ex-Glitter Band). Here he's just cooling off by resting on the bonnet — and causing quite a stir with the crowd!

In fact, now we come to think of it, most of the lads we know love to get behind a wheel at every possible opportunity — and it seems the stars aren't much different.

Once you get to be a superstar, there's no need for a bicycle! It's the excitement of the race-track and super-fast cars! Like Bay City Roller Eric says, "There's nothing like going at a 100 mph you feel you're flying!"

Film

BEN MURPHY ... Alias Jones, alias one of the tastiest guys ever to hit our telly screens!

ADAM FAITH Pop star ... now turned actor with lotsa success in Budgie, *also* That'll Be The Day.

TWIGGY About the most successful model ever — and now she's singing, dancing 'n' acting too!

RINGO STARR 'n' the lovely MIA FARROW.

Focus

... on some of your favourite screen personalities
— and one in particular!

We couldn't resist putting the spotlight on
the blond, blue-eyed and beautiful Robert
Redford. There's no doubt, this guy's just
about the tastiest actor to appear on the
silver screen in many a year!

WHAT with the rip-roaring Butch Cassidy, the beautiful 'The Way We Were', the excitement of 'The Sting' and that amazin' Gatsby style — it's not surprising our Rob's set so many hearts a-flutterin'!

But it wasn't just overnight success for Robert, y'know! There was many a long year of studying acting, and taking small film parts before he landed the role of 'The Kid' opposite the equally smashin' Paul Newman in Butch Cassidy. It was then, in '69, that he really hit the big-time. But, way back, before that? What's Rob's history, we wondered . . .

A REAL ARTIST

Well, not surprisingly, he's always been on the artistic side — but apparently, it took him quite a while to find his real vocation. As a kid he was always sketching (usually people, he says) so, when he grew up and left college in Colorado he took a trek all over Europe — staying in Florence and Paris to study painting.

And, of course, he enjoyed it — it was a wonderful time to look back on — even tho' he admits that he never really hit the big time as a painter. Now whenever he finds time to relax, painting remains one of the most pleasant pastimes to Rob — a talent he can really develop, at his leisure.

Soon he was making a slow but sure way back to America — back to the world he knew. It wasn't long before he knew what he *really* wanted to do — and began to study acting

wholeheartedly.

Of course, by now we've got a good idea of what Rob's like as an actor — he's our hero!

But what's he really like off-screen, this Redford fella? Well, he's a fantastic sporting guy — he likes riding and skiing. But first and foremost, it's the acting that matters.

"I want to be an actor — not a star," he says. Well, we reckon he's achieved both very nicely, thank you.

But since Robert set a foot on the road to stardom with Butch Cassidy, he's never looked back — every film he's starred in after that has been a rip-roaring success for him!

"I always try to push myself to the very limits, both physically and mentally, to discover what I'm really made of. If you don't push yourself and take risks you'll never know your own limits."

DAREDEVIL ROB!

And he's still pushing himself and receiving the success he deserves. In 'Waldo Pepper', he insisted on doing all the daredevil flying stunts himself. Brave, eh? Our blood runs cold at the thought of the risks he took. But for him they're all taken with a pinch of salt, it's just part of a day's work!

Very like the indomitable Mr. Steve McQueen, part of lovin' this star is knowin' that you just can't stop him from going on pushing himself until he reaches those limits.

But somehow we don't think that'll be for some time yet!

SHE-WOLF

Bill worked in a safari park — and it was a beautiful she-wolf who worried Carol . . .

TAKE IT EASY, CAROL! BILL KNOWS WHAT HE'S DOING!

DOES HE? SOMEHOW I DON'T TRUST THAT FEMALE WOLF HE'S SO FOND OF!

MAYBE I'M BEING CHILDISH! I DON'T GET JEALOUS OVER OTHER GIRLS! BUT I SOMETIMES WISH BIANCA WAS HUMAN — SO I COULD SCRATCH HER GREEN EYES OUT!

How Popular Are You?

Are you the kinda girl who everyone loves to have around? The girl who's at the top of everybody's party list? Is your social life just one exhausting round of fun . . . ? Or do you tend to sit home on your own most of the time, just waitin' for the telephone to ring? Do our quiz and find out just how you rate.

1 Well, for a kick-off, how many *real* friends do you reckon you have?
a. *Too numerous to mention! You have so many friends you lost count of them long ago!*
b. *You're really not too sure — but you could probably count them on the fingers of both hands . . . Maybe even one hand would be enough!*
c. *You know lots of people — but* real *friends? Sometimes you wonder if you have any at all.*

2 You see your best mate's boyfriend out with another girl and, judging by his guilty expression, you reckon this is no innocent friendship. So, what do you do about it?
a. *You wait for the first opportunity to get your friend on her own — then break it to her very gently.*
b. *You go straight to your friend and tell her what you saw . . . then you get all your friends on your side to convince her what a rotter her fella is and that she should have nothing more to do with him.*
c. *You keep what you saw to yourself. It's really none of your business, after all, and it would only upset your friend if she knew.*

3 When it comes to parties and things are you naturally the last person to leave?
a. *No. In fact, you're often one of the first . . . As soon as you sense that the peak is past and your hostess is beginnin' to look a bit tired, you reckon it's time to go.*
b. *Yeah, you gotta admit it, you are generally the last to call it a day. When they're goin' round pickin' up the empty coke bottles, you're still there, dancin' to the music.*
c. *You're not the last . . . nor the first. You just go with the rest when the party starts to break up.*

4 One of your schoolmates is in hospital after an appendix op. You reckon she must need a bit of cheering, so what do you do?
a. *You organise a whole gang of you to go to the hospital together one afternoon to lay on a spot of entertainment for her.*
b. *You go to see her with a couple of friends, taking some flowers and mags for her to read.*
c. *You keep thinking you'd like to go and visit her, but in the end you just send her a 'Get Well' card.*

5 You're invited round to a friend's house for Sunday lunch. Her mum provides a real spread and you have yourself a feast. When the meal's over what do you do?
a. *Help with the washing-up, naturally. That's the least you can do!*
b. *You feel a bit shy with your friend's family, so you just retire to a corner and read the Sunday papers.*
c. *Well, while your friend and her mum are clearing up, you entertain Dad and the brothers 'n' sisters with your repertoire of jokes and funny stories.*

6 You walk into the changing-room unexpectedly one day after a PE lesson and overhear some of your class-

mates saying some rather cruel thing about your best friend. What do you do?

a. *You just hope they didn't notice you come in — and quickly slip out the door again.*

b. *You barge in, defending your friend and demanding to know where they heard those stories from.*

c. *You don't say anything directly to them, but you let them know that you heard what they were saying and that you consider it a pack of nasty lies.*

7 Think about it . . . when it comes to gettin' together with your mates to listen to records 'n' things, does it

tend to be at their place — or yours?

a. *Mostly at your place, you reckon. You're always organising get-togethers.*

b. *About fifty-fifty. You try to take your share of the hostessin' bit.*

c. *You almost never have your mates round at your place. You prefer to be the guest.*

8 You've gone along to the sports club to watch your fella playin' for his team. After the game he invites you to meet some of his friends. How do you react?

a. *You say 'Yes, please!' It's a great chance for you to widen your circle of*

friends — and you're not one to miss an opportunity to do that!

b. *You tell him you'd really rather not meet them. You came to see him . . . and, really he's the only person you want to be with anyway.*

c. *Of course you want to meet them! And you're flattered that he wants to share his friends with you.*

1. a(10) b(5) c(0)
2. a(5) b(10) c(0)
3. a(0) b(10) c(5)
4. a(10) 5(5) c(0)
5. a(5) b(0) c(10)
6. a(0) b(10) c(5)
7. a(10) b(5) c(0)
8. a(10) b(0) c(5)

55—80
Well, we've got to hand it to you — you certainly work pretty hard at bein' popular! And you probably do have lots of friends. Beware, tho', that you don't sacrifice quality for quantity . . . you tend to collect friends like trophies — and that could put some people off!

25—50
We reckon you're a pretty popular girl . . . but, more important than that, you're really well-liked as well. You value your friends — you really care about them and their problems. Your friendships are the kind that last.

0—20
Well, you knew it anyway, didn't you? You're definitely not the most popular girl around! But why? Could be because you don't try hard enough. Have a bit more confidence in yourself, stop worrying about what other people are thinking about you all the time. Just have fun!

Lonely as Lisa

Lisa Caxton had become a puzzle to the people in the office where she worked . . .

HEY, LISA — LIKE TO COME DANCING TONIGHT?

NO THANKS. I'M BUSY!

LISA, DO YOU HAVE TO BE SO **COLD** WHEN YOU GIVE SOMEONE THE BRUSHOFF?

SORRY, SALLY, I HAVE **OTHER THINGS** TO THINK ABOUT!

WELL, IF YOU WON'T GO OUT WITH BOYS, COME OUT WITH US. WE'RE GOING TO THE PICTURES TONIGHT!

SORRY, SALLY. I **MEANT** WHAT I SAID. I REALLY **DO** HAVE OTHER THINGS TO DO!

107

Pink Solves Your Beauty Blues

don't and as far as colours go stick to light coloured pearly ones. If this is your first attempt try light blues and mauves. Once you've got the hang of it then try other colours. And also use lots of mascara — waterproof is the best bet.

MAX FACTOR LIP POTION ROLL-ON LIP SHINE

POLISH UP.
Dear Valli, I love wearing bright-coloured nail varnish but the problem is I'm right handed and can't seem to get the polish on my right hand properly — it goes all messy.
Can you help?

Gill, Surrey.

Dear Gill, Everybody seems to have this problem when they start using nail polish, and it does take practise.
But there are a few hints that will help.
Always paint your nails sitting at a table.
Put the hand you are painting flat on the table and rest the elbow of your painting arm, also on the table, this keeps both your hands steady and makes the

job that much easier.
Also make sure your brush isn't overloaded with polish, as then it's less likely to blob.
And lastly — most important —take your time!

THROUGH THE LOOKING GLASS
Dear Valli, I wear silver rimmed glasses and have blue eyes, the thing is I would like to wear some eye make-up but I'm not too sure what type I should choose — could you help me out?

Mary, Dundee.

Dear Mary, Eye make-up looks just as good on people who wear glasses as those who

SPOT CHECK
Dear Valli, Like lots of teenagers, I have a spot problem. Fortunately, though it's not too bad. Could you give me a basic routine for treating them?

Felicity, Notts.

Dear Felicity, I'm very glad that you accept your spots as a normal teenage complaint.
Many Pink readers write to me hoping that I can give them some miracle remedy to make their spots disappear. Well, as I'm sure many of you know by now,

there is no quick or sure answer to the spot problem.

What I can guarantee is that a scrupulous cleansing routine, with a sensible diet (steer clear of all fried and fatty food, sweet, stodgy things and go for plenty of fresh fruit—especially citrus—and green vegetables), will keep the spots down to a minimum. Another thing to remember, Felicity, is to keep your hair clean too (and always tie it away from your face when possible). Dirty, greasy hair only encourages spot infection. And never, never squeeze blackheads or spots you'll only bruise the skin and could even cause a scar. Be sure to always wash every trace of make-up and dirt off at night; clogging up your pores with stale make-up isn't going to help either.

Try and use a medicated soap,

like Clearasil and then a medicated astringent or cream, like D.D.D. And when you go out try using a spot stick, which covers your spot and does it good too. Rimmel do an excellent one called Hide the Blemish.

GUMMED UP

Dear Valli, My gums have been bleeding recently and I have heard conflicting stories as to whether this is good or bad. Could you straighten me out?
Valerie, Stafford.
Dear Valerie, A lot of people find that their gums bleed at one time or another, especially when they are brushing their teeth. There isn't usually anything to worry about but a check-up at the dentist will rest your mind either way. Don't worry though, the worst he can do is give you

a mouth wash and some medicine.

SORT IT OUT

Dear Valli, I wonder if you could sort out my problem, you see my friend says that you should have your hair cut every four to five months and I said it is more like four to five weeks. Who is right?
Helen, Manchester.
Dear Helen, You're nearer the mark in fact. The average space between haircuts should be six to eight weeks, it's the only way to keep your hair healthy, shining and manageable!

AND NOW
FOR SOMETHING COMPLETELY DIFFERENT

PINK ECCENTRICS

You may have heard of folk living in boxes, playing trains, being Red Indians and Cowboys and doing other eccentric things during their lives. Since our Jamie's rather an eccentric himself (who else would insist on going off to interview people in a donkey-drawn, balloon-assisted, home-made carriage on roller skates, propeller-driven?) we thought he might manage to recognise a few of his own kind . . .

THE PAPER ROLL COLLECTORS OF BRIDGE.

Mr. and Mrs. Finklesop live in a charming cottage. They seem quite normal folk, until you enter their house. Their place is packed with paper rolls of every colour, size and make. They just cannot collect enough of it.

Mr. Finklesop started in 1918 with his very first 'Bronco', and has been collecting ever since. As time went on, manufacturers produced more sophisticated rolls of paper — soft tissue; superstrong, mop-up kind, and then came the real heavy-duty stuff . . . you name it, Mr. Finklesop's got it — as he says, he has to move with the times. So the rooms of the house are packed with rolls and

rolls of paper. They are delighted with their collection and invited me to see it. It was an amazing sight.

I was particularly interested in an enormous pink roll of toilet tissue. But unfortunately it slipped from my hands and started rolling for the open door. Out it raced and down the street, unravelling as it went.

They weren't pleased, were the Finklesop's, not pleased at all.

THE LION TAMER OF TOOTING

Ramal Clanker is, as I was told, a famous lion-tamer. He will tame any lion, however fierce or dangerous it may be, the story goes. So I went in search of Mr.

Clanker and found him living in a house in Tooting.

An ordinary house until you opened the front door, and found yourself staring at thick iron bars as I did.

And I soon discovered that Ramal, as I was asked to call him, has bars at every window, doorway and mousehole in the house. He tames lions at home in his spare time. A huge roar came from the front room. I shuddered. A needless "Don't go in there" was said to me. I was shown right round the house. The roaring noise seemed to follow us wherever we went.

I was presented with a cup of tea and a piece of cake, and we sat down to chat. Suddenly the doorbell went, and I couldn't resist a little peek into the roaring room. I just *had* to see a real live lion. So I peeked through the crack in the door. The roaring was certainly very loud, but not from a lion. From a tape recorder. And there sitting in the middle of the room was this dear little black 'n' white cat.

Before I knew it Ramal had returned. I had opened the door wide and the cat was mewing towards me, licking its lips for the cream on my cake. Ramal went white with horror. "Leave that dangerous lion alone," he yelled. I jumped with fright, the cat jumped with fright, the tea toppled everywhere and as the door was slammed I was asked to leave. Funny fella.

THE HILL BILLIES OF HERNE HILL.

Believe it or not, there are Hill Billies in this country. They aren't American Hill Billies though, they are English ones. Two families of them. One family lives at number twelve Frigmore Avenue, the other family opposite at number thirteen. They HATE each other.

Off I went to visit them . . .

Both houses were surrounded by barbed wire, lots of it. The window's were shuttered at the front of each house. I went to number twelve first where the Harbuckles live.

Hesitantly, I knocked on the door. "If you are a friend of the Finchmores, you can go away,"

shouted a voice from inside. I explained who I was.

After a couple of groans, there was a sound of six bolts being drawn, the door opened a fraction and a beady eye looked me over. Suddenly the door was opened wide and I was dragged into the house. SLAM! the door was closed again and a lot of crashing and smashing came from the closed door as it was instantly bolted.

"Them Finchmores are firing their catapults again," said the little old lady dressed in tatty clothes who stood in front of me. "Nasty vicious folk," I was amazed.

Apparently the two families have been feuding for years, all over a pint of milk. The milkman delivered a pint to the Finchmores who said they didn't get it and accused the Harbuckles of stealing it. Fancy feuding over a bottle of milk.

Suddenly the back door opened and a man and two boys walked in carrying handfuls of conkers which they took upstairs. "Ammo," said the old lady. "We will teach those Finchmores a thing or two. Oh, yes!" With that she scampered upstairs.

I thought it was best to leave by the back door. So I did. Over the fence I nipped, just in time to hear a barrage of banging and crashing, cursing and screaming coming from the front of the house.

A young boy came out and guided me through his house to the street outside. "Don't tell anyone," he said. "But when my Dad was a boy, he stole a bottle of milk from the Finchmores when he was a lad. Funny, isn't it?" I had to admit it was rather funny.

THE MOLE MAN OF MORDEN

I have heard of people thinking they are Napoleon, David Cassidy, God and a few other famous people, but I have never heard of someone thinking that he was a MOLE. Living in Morden is just such a man.

I found out that he lived in Little Uckley Sidings, allotments number 12, 13, 14 and 15. So off I went to see the Mole Man of Morden.

I very soon found the right allotments, you couldn't really

miss them. They were covered in round heaps of earth. KEEP OUT. BURROWING — read the notice by a gate. I couldn't see anyone, so I called out. Silence. But then I detected a digging noise coming from the other side of the allotments. I went to investigate — as all good journalists do.

Carefully treading between piles of muddy earth, and narrowly missing going down a few holes, I reached the other side. I called again. Suddenly out of this hole crawled this very small man. He was dressed in a boiler suit and was wearing a pit helmet and carrying a huge pointed shovel. This was the Mole Man of Morden.

"Come and see me later," he said. "I can't stand the light. Come tonight." And with those few words, he vanished down the hole again, and lumps of earth came flying out.

I didn't return. Enough was enough. If I had gone back at night, there would have been two Mole Men of Morden. I would have surely walked straight into one of those holes!

THE BLOOMERS KNICKER OF KNIGHTSBRIDGE.

In a funny little house in Knightsbridge, lives a funny little man who, I am told, travels all over the country collecting bloomers off people's washing lines.

His fame has spread far and wide and his house is stuffed full of 'em. Danger being my middle name, I ventured to go and interview him.

He was pleased to see me and invited me into his front room. Where, as soon as I was seated, he showed me his prized possession — the biggest pair of bloomers I have ever seen.

"Belonged to Queen Vic.," he said rather proudly. I asked him why he collected bloomers (weren't they getting scarce these days?) and why he hadn't been knicked, I mean, arrested for taking them. He gave me a secret smile. The fact was, that he didn't really knick, sorry, steal the bloomers, no, he bought them. "I just love collecting them," he said. "Spend all my money on them." I left thinking there were better things to spend money on.

THE DEVIL MASK

I'm Denny Porter's girl. I do the costumes and make-up for Denny's group, the Devil's Disciples — and I thought it was all a load of fun until a very weird thing happened . . .

MM, MUST SAY DENNY AND THE BOYS LOOK GREAT TONIGHT — EVEN IF I DO SAY SO MYSELF!

I remember I felt a strange shudder as he picked up the mask to wrap it.

IT HAS A SMILE, A HORRIBLE, SNEERING GRIN — THE WAY DENNY LOOKS SOMETIMES!

I was glad to get outside, but then . . .

MY SCOOTER — IT'S GONE! AND THAT WEIRD SIGN ON THE PAVEMENT . . .

OH, DENNY, THANK HEAVENS IT'S YOU! SOMETHING HORRIBLE'S HAPPENED! THERE WAS THIS STRANGE DEVIL DESIGN ON THE PAVEMENT. MY SCOOTER — ITS. JUST DISAPPEARED!

OH DENNY, WHAT'S GOING ON? WHY DO I FEEL SOMETHING AWFUL'S GOING TO HAPPEN?

DEVIL, LISA? YOUR SCOOTER GONE? NOW WAIT, THE MARK WAS PROBABLY JUST SOMETHING KIDS HAVE SCRIBBLED! AND YOUR SCOOTER — WELL, THAT'S OVER THERE! DON'T YOU REMEMBER — YOU WALKED TO THE SHOP?

I DON'T KNOW, LOVE. BUT BELIEVE ME, EVERYTHING'S ALL RIGHT!

I POPPED IN TO SAY WE'LL NEED THOSE NEW OUTFITS BY TOMORROW! WE'VE GOT A CONCERT TO DO IN LONDON!

WOW! THEN I'D BETTER GET DOWN TO SOME WORK!

119

A doctor in the audience raced up behind the closed curtains — and the whole world seemed to stand still . . .

TELL ME . . . YOU'VE GOT TO TELL ME, DOCTOR, WHAT IT IS!

When Denny came to, the doctor told both uf us . . .

IT'S A WARNING . . . TO DENNY . . . AND TO YOU, LISA! DENNY COLLAPSED FROM OVERWORK, TOO MUCH STRAIN AND TENSION. HE'S GOT TO TAKE IT EASY FOR A WHILE, OR ELSE . . .

So THAT was it . . . the pressure of success . . . twisting Denny into someone I hardly knew at times . . . frightening me into a nightmare world of fear and wild imagination

AND YOU, MY GIRL . . . YOU LOOK AS IF YOU COULD DO WITH A BREAK FROM ALL THE WORRY. WHY DON'T YOU GET AWAY AND ENJOY YOURSELVES LIKE AN ORDINARY BOY AND GIRL FOR A CHANGE!

HE'LL TAKE IT EASY NOW, DOCTOR, BE-LIEVE ME!

IT DOESN'T SEEM POSSIBLE, DENNY, ON A BEAUTIFUL DAY LIKE THIS, THAT I REALLY IMAGINED YOU WERE IN THE GRIP OF THE DEVIL

MAYBE IN A WAY, I, WAS LOVE. DAY AND NIGHT, ONLY THINKING OF MORE SUCCESS . . . MORE FAME AND GLORY . . . MORE MONEY, MORE POWER

I THINK I FORGOT ABOUT THE THINGS . . . THAT REALLY MATTER!

THE END

AN EXCITING PINK SHORT STORT

Black Sultan

KAREN *suddenly woke up to the shouting voices and the terrified neighing of horses. She jumped out of bed to the window, a strange glow lit the room — FIRE. The stables were on fire, the new stables where her father, Sean Byron kept his prize show jumping horses. Men were running, carrying buckets of water to try and extinguish the fire. But they were fighting a loosing battle. Stable-hands were struggling with some of the terrified horses that were being led from the stables. Karen had to help!*

Quickly she dressed and hurried outside.

"Are all the horses safe?" she asked Bill Madox, the head trainer.

"No", he shook his head, "Black Sultan is still in there somewhere. He is going mad with terror. Won't let anyone near him. Can't get near him."

Black Sultan was the best horse Karen's father owned. But he had a savage streak in him, Karen was the only person who could really control him, but would he, in his terror, let the girl near him — to save his life?

"I must go to him," gasped Karen, running towards the blazing stables.

Sean saw his daughter's haste. He ran after her, grabbing her arm. "You can't go in there! No one can," he shouted. Karen struggled free and ran into the blazing building, all she could think of was Black Sultan's terrified screams.

The smoke was thick inside the stable, Karen didn't stop her pace. She knew exactly where Black Sultan was.

"I'm here, Sultan, I'm here!," she shouted. The horse seemed to calm, but couldn't keep still. Her eyes streaming, Karen reached the huge black horse. The stable door catch was very stiff, Karen looked desperately round for something to ease it open with. Black Sultan was getting nervous and restless again, his eyes bulging with fright. Karen knew she would have to be quick.

She grabbed a hoof pick and working desperately managed to prise the catch apart. Karen was coughing and could hardly see, her strength was going fast, she felt light-headed and dizzy. Quickly she threw herself on to Black Sultan's back, "Go, boy, go," she screamed. The horse needed no more help, no more instructions. He was off, galloping out into the clear night air, taking Karen with him.

As soon as the great horse was outside, his panic left him, and he stopped near Sean. Karen lay groggily across the horse's back.

"That was a stupid and dangerous thing to do," said Sean, helping his daughter down. "You could have been killed."

One of the stable hands brought a glass of water, Karen gratefully took a drink. The fire engines' sirens could be heard coming towards the stables.

Karen, gulping down air, soon felt better. She looked lovingly at Black Sultan standing there, held by Bill. "It was worth the risk I took, Dad," she said. "Black Sultan is the only horse likely to win the Bradmore Gold Cup next Saturday."

Bill led Black Sultan off to the other stables and Karen went to bed. There was nothing else to do, the fire brigade were doing their best, but the stables were nearly burnt to the ground.

The smell of burnt wood hung over the stables, and Karen could smell it all over the house. There was no one in the kitchen — where was Mum and Dad? . . . In the study. They'd probably be getting in touch with the insurance company. She passed the study door, a raised voice could be heard, "What do you mean? The insurance ran out last month? Not been paid?"

Karen's heart missed a beat. How could her Dad continue with half his stables burnt to the ground? He hadn't been doing all that well lately. This could finish him and his stables. Selling the best horses would be the only answer — that meant selling Black Sultan!

She went into the study. Her father was putting down the telephone. His face was ashen. Mother was sitting in the arm-chair, looking faint and frightened. "I'm finished," sighed

122

Sean. "There is just nothing I can do. How did I forget to pay that Insurance? We must have new stables for the horses. They can't live in the old stables for long. Too damp and rotten."

"But if Black Sultan wins the Jumping on Saturday, the prize money will pay for new stables," said Karen.

Her father looked dubious. "Yes, you are right," he said. "But Black Sultan has *got to win!*" And it is the first time you have ridden on him in a competition. You are the only person here, he will let ride him."

Through the window, Karen could see the firemen searching through the smoking embers.

"Why are they searching, father? she asked going over to the window. "Surely there is nothing else they can do."

"Oh, I forgot to tell you," said Sean grimly. "The fire chief suspects arson."

The firemen stopped searching and were studying a piece of burnt timber. One of them got up and came over to the house.

In the study Karen and her parents were informed that the fire had been started deliberately!

"We are positive this is a case of arson," said the fire chief. "I don't suppose you have any idea who it could be who started this fire? Anyone with a grudge perhaps? Have you fired anyone lately?"

Karen's father shook his head. "I cannot think of anyone who works for me who would do such a terrible thing," he said. "No one I know would endanger the lives of horses in this way."

But someone had!

The police were called in and all the staff were questioned. Every one of them could tell the police where they were when the fire had started.

Karen was sick of the whole affair and went to see Black Sultan. The horse cantered over to her from the field he had been put in. He nuzzled her gently, as if to thank her for saving his life.

"We must win the competition on Saturday, Sultan," sighed Karen, tears filling her eyes. "We must win, or you will have to be sold with the other horses."

Just then there was a crunching of tyres on the gravel drive.

Karen turned to see Rodney Banks and his father get out of their Landrover. The Banks were Sean's neighbours, they owned stables too. The best horses for miles were bred there.

Rodney's father went into Karen's house. Rodney came over to the girl.

"Still going to compete against me on Saturday then?" smirked Rodney. "You don't stand a chance you know."

"Oh, go away," said Karen. "Wait until Saturday and you will see. Black Sultan is the finest jumper my father has ever had, you and your father know it. We will win, not you!"

Just then Rodney's father appeared with Sean. Karen's father looked angry. "Think it over," Mr. Banks was saying. "You are upset now. But mine is the best offer you will receive. Sell to me now. I might not be so charitable next week."

Rodney ran back to his father, and off they went.

"What is it, Dad?" called Karen running over. "What did Mr. Banks want?"

"He offered to buy Black Sultan," said Sean. "Somehow he knows about the insurance and the trouble I am in. Goodness knows how. But he does."

Sean turned and went indoors. Karen felt sorry for her father. But things would be all right after the horse jumping competition, after she and Sultan had won it!

The night before the competition, Karen went to bed early. She lay there thinking about the great day ahead of her. Hoping she would win, knowing Black Sultan would do his best. She was just dozing off when she heard neighing coming from the old stables. Surely not fire again!

Karen leaped from her bed and looked out into the night. No tell-tale smoke or glow. But it was certainly Black Sultan making the noise. Something was upsetting him.

Karen put her dressing gown on, her father met her on the landing and they went out together.

Hurrying to the stables as fast as they could, Sultan was upsetting the other horses. But where was Bill Madox? He was supposed to be with the horses tonight.

Karen and her father went into the stables. The lights were on, the horses seemed to calm down at their appearance. Bill was not in sight. Karen hurried to Black Sultan, he was sweating as if something had frightened him. A thump and a groan behind her made Karen turn, her father was slumping to the floor, Rodney Banks was standing there with a piece of wood in one hand, a gun in the other.

"One sound," he said, "and your horse will be killed."

Karen stifled a scream. Black Sultan started stamping his feet, pawing the earth. "What do you want?" said Karen.

"Lead that horse outside with me, don't make a sound," said Rodney. "The brute tried to kick me."

Karen knew she would have to do as she was told. Carefully she unhitched Black Sultan and led him outside.

"There is a horse-box down the road, follow me there," Rodney told the frightened girl.

Karen and Black Sultan were put into the horse-box and shut in together. Suddenly they found themselves moving along – and fast too. But where were they going, and why were they being kidnapped? What had happened to Bill Madox?

AFTER what seemed like hours, the horse-box stopped. The side door was opened and Rodney looked in.

"You can stay here now," he said. "By the time you are found, I will have won the competition, got the money and left the country. Your horse was too good for any of my poor father's."

The door was slammed and another motor started and drove off into the distance. Karen sat on the floor, wondering what to do. How could she and Black Sultan get away and go to the competition?

In the darkness, Karen went into a troubled sleep. She was woken by Black Sultan nuzzling her. Light filtered through the gaps in the horse-box and she could see around in the dim light.

Karen tried to open the door. But it wouldn't move. Perhaps the back part would be easier. But no. It was locked tight.

She heard a scratching noise coming from the roof. Suddenly

Continued on page 124

BLACK SULTAN

Continued from page 123

sne remembered something, some horse-boxes have flaps at the top to let in air if the weather is very hot. How could she get up there? Black Sultan was the answer. Karen could just reach the roof by standing on his back. But would he stay still enough for her to do that?

Karen climbed on to his back and stood up. It wasn't easy but she could just reach the roof. She pushed. Something moved, but it was very stiff. Karen pushed again, the opening moved a bit more. Suddenly Black Sultan moved, just as Karen was pushing again, the flap opened, and sunlight poured in. Pushing on the side of the horse-box, Karen clambered out of the opening. She was free!

CLIMBING down the outside was easy. And soon she had opened the horse-box and was leading Black Sultan out.

But where were they? Where had Rodney left them? There was a derelict farmhouse not far away. Suddenly Karen realised that they were just ten miles away from the stables. She and Black Sultan sure had to move fast if they were going to compete in the Bradmore Gold Cup. In a second, Karen was up onto the great horse's back and off they galloped, over fields and pastures.

After a hard ride, the stables came in sight. She could see a police car and people by the stables. Karen galloped on.

Sean turned his bandaged head and saw Karen and Black Sultan racing towards them.

"Are we too late?" puffed Karen stopping Black Sultan. "The competition hasn't started yet, has it?"

Her father smiled with relief. "No, there is a couple of hours to go yet, where have you been? We've been out of our minds with worry," he said.

Karen went indoors and told the story. "I am sure it was Rodney who started the fire," she said.

"Well, the police will soon catch up with him," said Sean.

"His father can't know about his son, surely."

Sultan was given a feed and after a couple of hours, he and Karen went to the competition.

There the family met a policeman.

"We haven't found Rodney yet," explained the constable. "His father says he hasn't seen him since this morning. But he can't have gone far. Don't worry we will find him Mr. Byron."

After hearing that Rodney was still free, Karen felt a bit worried. He was a very dangerous man. The strangest thing of all though, was that Bill Madox hadn't been seen . . .

Karen was the last contestant to jump. No one had cleared the course when it came to her turn. One of Mr. Bank's riders was in the lead with only four faults.

"The next contestant is Karen Byron riding Black Sultan," said the announcer's voice over the loudspeaker.

Out into the arena rode Karen, Black Sultan holding his head up proudly. Over the first jump cleanly, Black Sultan jumping it with ease. Twelve more jumps to do. The horse seemed to be so happy and at ease as he went for each jump. Karen rode him beautifully.

The last jump but one ahead, a clear round so far. Suddenly there was a scuffling in the crowd round the arena and a man raced out in front of Karen — it was Rodney Banks. Even though he couldn't possibly ride or win the competition, he didn't want Karen to win it either. Suddenly another person broke from the crowd and raced towards Rodney — it was Bill, Billy Madox.

Karen felt Black Sultan hesitate, Rodney was putting him off completely.

"I must jump over Rodney," thought Karen. She dug her heels in the horse's flank, just as Bill knocked Rodney to the ground, Black Sultan leaped over the fighting pair. But now his stride was wrong for the next fence. Could he clear it? He would have to jump it too early. Well, Karen would just have to take that chance!

Black Sultan took off, stretching himself towards the fence, flying through the air, Karen hanging on grimly.

Up, up, over. A rattle as Black Sultan's hind feet touched the fence. Had the bar been knocked over? Karen had another fence to jump, she couldn't look back. It was the highest fence on the course. Could Black Sultan manage it? The horse seemed determined, using all the power he had he leaped for the fence. A roar rose from the crowd as Black Sultan cleared the last fence. But had Karen won?

Her heart seemed to stop, waiting for the announcement to come . . .

"The only clear round of the competition has been achieved by Karen Byron, riding Black Sultan," said the announcer.

Karen had won. Black Sultan had won!

Proudly Sean went out to congratulate his daughter.

The police were leading Rodney Banks away, and Bill Madox was running over to Karen and Black Sultan.

"Thank goodness I got here in time", said Bill. "I suspected Rodney was behind all this some days ago. But he managed to lock me up. I got free though — just in time!"

KAREN wasn't worried about Rodney any more though, Black Sultan had won the competition, and with the prize money, her father could start again.

Suddenly a policeman came up and put his hand on Bill's shoulder. "Would you come along with me, sir?" he said. "We have reason to believe that you are responsible for the fire at Mr. Byron's stables."

Bill was led away. So there were more surprises to come . . . It was true, Karen found out later. Mr. Banks needed to win the competition more than Karen's father had, so he had got Bill to start the fire to finish Karen's father's chances of winning. But that was over.

Things were all right once more, thanks to Black Sultan.

GROWING PAINS

Dear Chris, I'm eleven and just recently have been really depressed about my problem.

You see, my bust has started growing and I'm the first girl in my form to start developing a bust.

I often get a lot of discomfort — itching, particularly — at the most awkward times like during lessons, and as I go to a mixed school this is doubly embarrassing.

The other day I noticed that each breast has a hard lump in it and this is really worrying me. Don't tell me to talk to my mum about this as, when I asked her if I could have a bra because my bust was hurting me she just said, "Oh, don't be ridiculous — at your age." And I felt so embarrassed I could have died.

I've got a sister who's sixteen but she's always off out with her friends.

What should I do?

Paula, Luton.

Dear Paula, Firstly let me put your mind at rest about these 'lumps' and the itching you speak of. Both these are natural signs that your bust has started to develop. The lumps, or 'hard cores' won't always be there. They will disappear naturally when your bust starts getting bigger.

As for the itching — well we all get a tingling and itchy feeling in our muscles when we've been active . . . this just means the breast muscles are reacting to change. I agree it is embarrassing when you experience this without relief. But why not excuse yourself from class until the discomfort passes? — no one need know why.

Since you mention that you're the first girl in your class to visibly start developing her bust, this is probably why your mum feels it's so soon to start talking of such things as bras. Nevertheless, a girl can start growing her bust at any age — and your mum should understand that if you would feel much happier and more comfortable wearing some support, then you should be able to.

Why not have a word with your sister — after all, she must have

It takes a lot of courage to write and tell someone about a personal problem — something that you feel too embarrassed to face anybody about. Well, I receive a lot of your personal worries — here's just two which have cropped up repeatedly over the past year . . .

experienced this too. Explain that you feel very embarrassed at school not wearing a bra. I'm sure she'll understand and explain your feelings more seriously to your mum.

However, if all else fails, why not ask for advice from one of the women teachers at school — she'll be able to make your mum see things as they are.

PERIODS

Dear Chris, I had my period for the first time three months ago and haven't had it since. I'm really worried about this but am too shy to ask my Mum about it and I don't want to go to a doctor.

Would you explain about periods and what I should expect, as no one I know ever has, and I'm mixed up about it.

Catherine, Kent

Dear Catherine, I keep receiving lots of letters just like yours, so I thought this was as good a time as any to tackle this question again.

As to your particular query, although it's always best to check with a doctor when puzzled about anything physical, I don't think there's much for you to worry about. Some girls are very irregular when they begin to menstruate — that is they might have their periods once, then wait a few more months before the next one. Usually, they regularize themselves after a time, but there are cases where girls continue to have irregular periods their whole lives.

Menstrual periods are natural — and normal — the signal that womanhood is in the offing. So we should actually look forward to this time in our lives. It's nature's way of saying we're on our way!

What actually happens is that the body gets rid of excess blood it stores each month along with a tiny, tiny egg, tinier than a dot you could make with the sharpest pencil point. Another way of saying it is that it's a purifying action because the body is ridding itself of something it doesn't need.

The average cycle is about every 28 days, but everyone is different, so there are really no rules. Often, you have to wait a while before knowing what your particular cycle is — that is, how often you'll have your period. Some are regular, others aren't. Some girls begin their periods when they're young — 10 or 11; others, at an older age — 15, 16, 17. But one is as normal as the next, just different.

When you begin to have them quite regularly, it's a good idea to keep a record of when your periods begin and end by circling the dates on a calendar. Then you'll know when to expect them and be prepared.

After a while, you begin to know without a calendar. You might feel a bit tired or heavier just beforehand, and sometimes be rather emotional.

Now, this is the general view. As I said, there are always exceptions, but no matter what category you happen to be in, you can be sure that having your period is just a simple, normal, natural part of life.

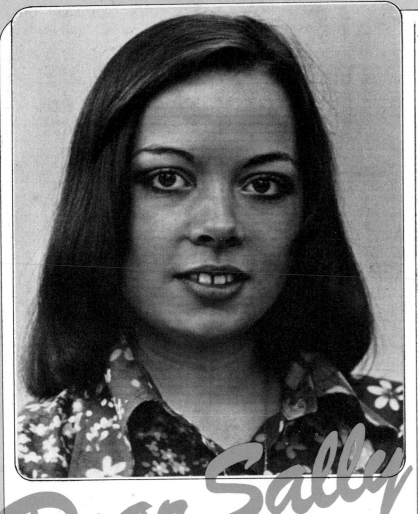

Dear Sally

Spring, summer, winter, autumn — problems are the same all year round, and it doesn't much matter what part of the world you happen to be in. We all have ups and downs. So write to me — won't you? — whenever you're troubled . . .

SO DEPRESSING

Dear Sally, I'm feeling so depressed. You see, I'm all alone most of the time and have no one to go around with outside of school. I've tried going out and enjoying myself, but that just hasn't worked.

A few weeks ago, I went to a disco, but all I did was sit in a corner looking like a dodo. It was one big waste of money and time.

Please help. I'm 15.

Susan, London

Dear Susan, I know that being alone is far from being fun, but it does have its rewards, even though,

at the moment, you can't see it that way. As far as I'm concerned, for example I'd rather be alone than be with a bunch of people just for the sake of company.

Why is this? Because at least when you're by yourself, you can be yourself.

You strike me as someone who is very sensitive and therefore, the friends you need should be equally as sensitive. Now, even if you found one such friend, you'd be lucky. It often takes a long time to form a deep friendship, and it's not always easy.

Trying to follow the crowd just

for the sake of it doesn't seem to go with your nature, and it's really much better to act according to your own nature rather than to try to be like everyone else. Better, but difficult.

So until you can click with another girl (and really, this'll happen so suddenly you won't even know it!), try to be content with yourself. If you're able to reach this contentment, you won't have to look for friends. They'll come looking for you.

BLUSHES

Dear Sally, Please help me. I blush at the least little thing. If a boy I like walks past me, I blush — or even if a teacher talks to me in school.

I've tried everything, like taking deep breaths and thinking of pleasant things, but this just doesn't work. I can't bear the thought of looking like a beetroot the rest of my life.

Janine, Australia

Dear Janine, Blushing is merely a symptom of not expressing something you feel. Somewhere inside you, you feel ashamed to show the real you — so you blush.

Often, though, instead of fighting something, it's better to give in, to surrender, to "go with it." And I think this just may be the case with you right now.

So when you feel yourself beginning to blush, let it happen, and say to yourself, "So I'm blushing. What's the big deal?" You can even say out loud, "Oh, excuse me. I always blush. That's the way I am."

When you're able to bring this out into the open, you'll feel less embarrassed, and so will others.

And, in time, you'll find that you have nothing to blush about. Even if you do, it won't bother you in the slightest.

NOT SURE OF HIM

Dear Sally, I've gone out for three months with a boy I really like very much. The trouble is, he only asks me out when there's no one